Essential
Costa
del Sol

by Mona King

PASSPORT BOOKS
NTC/Contemporary Publishing Company

Above: *an Andalusian*

Page 1: *a bar in Marbella*

Page 5a: *locals on a balcony*
5b: *a bull advertizes sherry*

Page 15a: *Patio de Mexuar, La Alhambra, Granada*
15b: *carving in Vélez-Málaga's town hall door*

Page 27a: *Alcazár gardens, Córdoba*
27b: *sculpture, Torremolinos*

Page 91a: *Nerja beach*
91b: *at Fuengirola*

Page 117a: *Fuengirola harbor*
117b: *A matador, Mijas*

This edition first published in 2000 by Passport Books, a division of NTC/ Contemporary Publishing Group, Inc., 4255 West Touhy Avenue, Lincolnwood (Chicago), Illinois 60712–1975 U.S.A.

Revised second edition 2000
Copyright © The Automobile Association 1998, 2000
Maps © The Automobile Association 1998

The contents of this publication are believed correct at the time of printing. Nevertheless, the publishers cannot accept responsibility for errors or omissions, nor for changes in details given. We are always grateful to readers who let us know of any errors or omissions they come across, and future printings will be updated accordingly.

Published by Passport Books in conjunction with The Automobile Association of Great Britain.

Written by Mona King

Library of Congress Catalog Card Number: on file
ISBN 0-658-00629-0

Color separation: BTB Digital Imaging, Whitchurch, Hampshire

The weather chart on **page 118** of this book is calibrated in °C. For conversion to °F simply use the following formula:
$$°F = 1.8 \times °C + 32$$

Printed and bound in Italy by Printer Trento srl

Contents

About this Book 4

Viewing Costa del Sol 5–14
Mona King's Costa del Sol	6
Costa del Sol's Features	7
Essence of Costa del Sol	8–9
The Shaping of Costa del Sol	10–11
Peace and Quiet	12–13
Costa del Sol's Famous	14

Top Ten 15–26
La Alcazaba, Málaga	16
La Alhambra, Granada	17
Casares	18
Cuevas de Nerja	19
La Giralda and La Catedral, Sevilla	20
Marbella's Casco Antiguo	21
La Mezquita, Córdoba	22
Mijas	23
Puerto Banús	24–5
Ronda's Puente Nuevo	26

What To See 27–90
Málaga	28–39
Costa del Sol and Beyond	40–90
In the Know	54–5
Food and Drink	72–3

Where To... 91–116
Eat and Drink	92–97
Stay	98–101
Shop	102–5
Take the Children	106–7
Be Entertained	108–16

Practical Matters 117–24

Index 125–6

Acknowledgements 126

About this Book

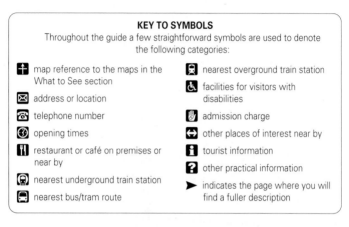
Essential *Costa del Sol* is divided into five sections to cover the most important aspects of your visit to Costa del Sol.

Viewing Costa del Sol pages 5–14

An introduction to Costa del Sol by the author
Costa del Sol's Features
Essence of Costa del Sol
The Shaping of Costa del Sol
Peace and Quiet
Costa del Sol's Famous

Top Ten pages 15–26

The author's choice of the Top Ten attractions in Costa del Sol, with practical information.

What to See pages 27–90

Two sections: Málaga and Costa del Sol & Beyond, each with brief introductions and an alphabetical listing of the main attractions
Practical information
Snippets of 'Did You Know…' information
4 suggested walks
4 suggested tours
2 features

Where To... pages 91–116

Detailed listings of the best places to eat, stay, shop, take the children and be entertained.

Practical Matters pages 117–24

A highly visual section containing essential travel information.

Maps

All map references are to the individual maps found in the What to See section of this guide.

For example, the town of Casares has the reference ✚ 46A1 – indicating the page on which the map is located and the grid square in which the town is to be found. A list of the maps that have been used in this travel guide can be found in the index.

Prices

Where appropriate, an indication of the cost of an establishment is given by **£** signs:

£££ denotes higher prices, **££** denotes average prices, while **£** denotes lower charges.

Star Ratings

Most of the places described in this book have been given a separate rating:

✪✪✪	Do not miss
✪✪	Highly recommended
✪	Worth seeing

Viewing
Costa
del Sol

Mona King's Costa del Sol   6
Costa del Sol's Features   7
Essence of Costa del Sol   8–9
The Shaping of Costa
  del Sol   10–11
Peace and Quiet   12–13
Costa del Sol's Famous   14

Mona King's Costa del Sol

The Early Days

The first signs of tourism along this coast can be traced back to the early 19th century when the English discovered Málaga as a winter resort. However, it was at Torremolinos that the first hotels were built. The founding of the Marbella Club by Prince Alfonso von Hohenlohe of Liechtenstein played a key role in opening up the area to the jet set, putting it clearly on the social map. With its appeal to both the package tour market and the more discerning individual, the Costa del Sol has never looked back.

For many, mention of the Costa del Sol conjures up visions of suntanned bodies on the beach, luxurious hotels set in tropical gardens, golfing and glitzy marinas lined with millionaires' yachts, lively restaurants and swinging discos – in other words, the high life, where you might rub shoulders with celebrities. Indeed, the Costa del Sol can offer all of this though, since its popularity took off in the 1960s and it became the 'in place' for the jet set, it has had its ups and downs. Right now it is enjoying a revival.

The ambience is decidedly cosmopolitan and expatriates from all walks of life have settled here with a particularly high concentration around Torremolinos, Marbella and Fuengirola. The estimated figure for foreigners who live here, whether permanently or part-time, is over 100,000, mostly British, German, Dutch and Scandinavian.

Although the scene has changed with the times, the 'beautiful people' still come here. The tendency is now to seek more seclusion, however, with much of the entertaining and partying taking place in private. But the Costa del Sol still exudes an aura of glamour, which serves as a continuing magnet to visitors. Its mild, sunny winter climate, unrivalled in Europe, is an additional attraction.

In recent years there has been an effort to encourage visitors to look beyond the beach-only holiday, and to sample the more rural pleasures of the hinterland. The Costa del Sol is an excellent gateway to the beautiful interior of Andalucía with its enchanting white towns and villages dotted about the countryside, peaceful landscapes and its real jewels, the historic cities of Sevilla, Córdoba and Granada.

The popular holiday resort of Fuengirola has a special appeal for families

6

Costa del Sol's Features

Geography
• The Costa del Sol is now officially within the province of Málaga, but this book covers a more extended area, including the provinces of Málaga, Granada and Cádiz.
• The Costa del Sol covers nearly 300km of the Mediterranean coast.

Climate
• Average temperatures: spring 20°C, summer 28°C, autumn 18°C, winter 13°C.
• Average sea temperatures: 15°C in January, 24°C in August.
• A minimum 8 hours' sunshine is expected daily for 320 days a year.
• Most rainfall is likely to occur between December and March.

Agriculture
• The famous sweet Málaga wines are produced in Los Montes de Málaga Antequera, north of the city, and in La Axarquiá, to the east.
• Olive groves are a feature of the Andalucían landscape. Olive oil, which is refined in Málaga, rates among Spain's leading exports.
• Oranges and bananas, and acres of vegetables such as peppers, tomatoes and potatoes are cultivated along with wheat, sugarcane, tobacco and cotton.
• Cumin, coriander, cinnamon, marjoram, thyme and rosemary are among the herbs which flourish here.
• The uplands of the Guadalquivir are famous for black fighting bulls and thoroughbred horses.

Sport and Leisure
• Long sandy beaches stretch along the western Costa del Sol; east of Málaga you will come across smaller beaches and rocky coves.
• The Costa del Sol has some 46 golf courses.
• There are some 20 tennis clubs and many top-grade hotels have tennis courts.
• This stretch of coast boasts over 30 marinas (pleasure craft harbours) with plans for more underway.
• Many resorts offer sailing, waterskiing, windsurfing (top spot Punta de Tarifa) and scuba diving.
• Para-sailing, hang-gliding and delta-winging are also widely available in resorts.
• Skiing in the Sierra Nevada, Europe's most southerly ski resort, is a newly developed wintersport.
• Stables offer horse rides along and behind the coast.

Far from the crowded resorts, life in the rural areas continues in the old traditional ways

Spices
When the Moors first arrived on the Iberian peninsula, they found the land poorly cultivated, lacking in fruit and other produce. Under the Omeya, the ruling class, dams, irrigation canals and water mills were built. Pepper, cinnamon, coriander and cumin were among the spices which were introduced, soon to spread to the medieval courts of Europe. Spices were highly valued for their preservative and medicinal properties.

Essence of Costa del Sol

Life on the Costa del Sol is generally a relaxing affair with priorities leaning towards sunbathing, swimming (perhaps), drinking and eating, with a siesta occupying the greater part of the afternoon. The more energetic may want to go sailing or water-skiing, while others might opt for golf or tennis. In the evening, after a late dinner, the dedicated will enjoy dancing in a discotheque until the early hours.

Above: *goats corralled on a hillside near Torrox*

Right: *seafront fishing boats of Torre del Mar*

Below: *Sevilla and Málaga are popular with flamenco fans*

THE 10 ESSENTIALS

If you only have a short time to visit Costa del Sol, or would like to get a really complete picture of the region, here are the essentials:

• **Do the daytime scene** in Puerto Banús. Linger over a drink at the Sinatra Bar and admire the yachts. Join the celebrities and have lunch at one of the fashionable open air restaurants.

• **Enjoy fresh seafood** at any one of the *chiringuitos* (beach restaurants) in La Carihuela, Torremolinos.

• **Wander around** the picturesque old town of Marbella and end up having a drink in the Plaza de los Naranjos.

• **Visit Málaga** and do an evening round of the wealth of *tapas* bars centred in the old town.

• **Walk up to the Alcazaba and Gibralfaro** for the panoramic views over Málaga and the bay.

• **See a flamenco show** in Málaga or inland in Sevilla.

• **Have an evening drink** on Marbella's promenade and watch the sunset, taking in a wide view of the Rock of Gibraltar and coastline of Africa.

• **Do the rounds of Banús by night.** The action starts around midnight and continues until dawn

with dozens of discos, bars and clubs. Take your pick!

• **Drive up into the hills** to picturesque Mijas and enjoy the magnificent views.

• **Visit Ronda** to admire its stunning setting and famous old bridge, subject of countless paintings and photographs.

• **Highlights** include visits to the Alhambra in Granada, the great Mosque at Córdoba and Sevilla, capital of Andalucía.

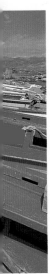

Top right: *Plaza de la Constitución, Fuengirola*

Right: *the dazzling image of Puerto Banús*

Left: *rooftops of old Antequera*

The Shaping of Costa del Sol

c25,000 BC
Paintings discovered in Nerja and Pileta caves show evidence of cave dwellers during this period.

4000 BC
Neolithic tribes from North Africa settle in southern Spain.

500 BC
The region is colonised by the Carthaginians.

210 BC
Following Roman domination, Andalucía is named Baetica. Málaga and Córdoba develop into important Roman towns.

AD 400
Decline of Roman Empire. The region is invaded by Vandals from northern Europe and named Vandalusia.

711
Moorish troops under the command of Tariq land in the south of Spain and begin the conquest of the peninsula. Moslem rule follows.

756
Al Andalus is converted into an emirate.

The flight of King Alfonso XIII in 1931 gave rise to the establishing of Spain's Second Republic

929
The independence of the Caliphate of Córdoba is proclaimed.

1031
The Caliphate is broken up into *tarifas* (small kingdoms).

1212
Christian victory at Las Navas de Tolosa (Jaén) marks a significant step in the reconquest of Andalucía.

1487
Armies of the Catholic Monarchs, Ferdinand and Isabella, conquer Málaga.

1492
Surrender of Granada to the Catholics ends Moorish rule in Spain. Banishment of Muslims and Jews.

1568
King Philip II takes measures against the Moriscos (Moors converted to Christianity) living in Málaga, who rebel and take refuge in the region of Las Alpujarras.

1610
Final expulsion of the Moriscos.

1808
The citizens of Málaga form a council to resist the French invaders, but the French advance and sack the city.

1812
The French are driven from Spain.

1873
Anarchy in Málaga. Attempts to set up an independent canton fail and the city is subdued by the government. The second half of the 19th century sees the emergence of an

affluent bourgeoisie and the building of grand properties.

1931
The departure from Spain of King Alfonso XIII sparks off unrest in Málaga; anarchy prevails.

1936
Uprising leads to the outbreak of civil war. The Nationalists take control of Sevilla, Córdoba, Granada. Málaga remains in the hands of the government.

1937
Málaga is taken by Nationalist forces.

1939
End of civil war with victory for General Franco; a period of hardship and poverty for the region over the next decade.

1950s
The start of investment in the Costa del Sol and the beginnings of mass tourism.

1982
Andalucía becomes one of Spain's 17 autonomous regions.

1985
The border with Gibraltar is reopened.

Tiles in Sevilla depicting the Christian Reconquest of Málaga

1992
Expo '92 held in Sevilla.

1997
Following a slump in tourism, a new era opens for the Costa del Sol. An ambitious investment programme, which includes the construction of new marinas and coastal promenades, golf courses and hotels, and improvements to the beaches, is giving a much-needed facelift to the area.

11

Peace & Quiet

For those who feel like taking a break from the hustle and bustle of the Costa del Sol, there are many possibilities. The hinterland offers a variety of landscapes, from olive groves in rolling hills, to dramatic mountain ranges with snowcapped peaks. In a very short time you can leave behind the heat of the coast and lose yourself in the tranquil surroundings of inland Andalucía.

The Coto de Doñana National Park is an important resting area for a great variety of migratory birds

Nature Parks and Reserves

Within reach of the coast are a number of protected areas and nature parks. With landscapes of wild natural beauty and a wealth of flora and fauna they make an ideal destination for the nature lover seeking peace and quiet.

Among these are the Parque Natural Montes de Málaga, north of Málaga; and south of Antequera, the Parque Natural Torcal de Antequera, which features weird and wonderful rock formations. Further west, from the Marbella area, you can easily reach the National Game Reserve near Monda, or the Parque Natural Sierra de Las Nieves, south of Ronda, with its rugged cliffs and great ravines.

Further west are the nature parks of Grazalema and Los Alcornocales, both areas of natural, unspoilt landscape. Southeast of Granada and easily accessible from the eastern section of the Costa del Sol is the Parque Natural Sierra Nevada, famed for its striking scenery and wealth of flora and fauna.

Green Tourism

The concept of green tourism is being developed by the regional government of Andalucía. The idea is to create an awareness of the countryside, allowing whole families to observe animals and plants in their natural habitat, enjoy home cooking and have contact with local people. A selection of accommodation offers this type of holiday and information can be obtained from: R A A R (Red Andaluza de Alojamientos Rurales), Apartado 2035, 04080 Almería ☎ 951 26 50 18.
Villas Turísticas, a new project of Turismo Andaluz, consists of groups of tourist villas in parks and remote areas of scenic landscapes. For more information contact: Turismo Andaluz, 29600 Marbella ☎ 952 83 87 85.

Hiking and Horseriding

The nature parks are wonderful areas for hikers and usually have marked trails for visitors to follow. Information on walking trails can be obtained from local tourist offices. The region of Las Alpujarras with its varied scenery also provides excellent walking terrain.

With its long tradition of raising and riding horses, Andalucía provides an ideal backdrop for long distance trekking. Stables are plentiful and horses can be hired to explore the coast and its hinterland.

Rural Accommodation

Mountain refuges and country houses in traditional Andalucían style make it possible to stay in some of these remote areas. Often located in wild, mountainous terrain and offering magnificent views, they are usually located near access roads.

Birdwatching

Spring and autumn are good periods to watch the European bird migration. Using Spain's southern coast as a resting place, hundreds of species of birds stop here on their journey between Africa and northern Europe. Early morning is a good time to see new arrivals and vantage points are Punta Marroquí at Tarifa, Calahonda, east of Marbella, and Benálmadena.

The nature reserve at the mouth of the river Guadalhorce, located just east of Torremolinos, not far from Málaga airport, is another good place for birdwatching. An area of exceptional beauty, however, is the Laguna de Fuente de Piedra. Located off the N334, west of Antequera, it is known as the Pink Lagoon, after the large colony of pink flamingos which comes here every year to breed. The best time to see these spectacular birds is from the end of January to June.

Las Alpujarras
Lying between the coastal sierras of Lujar, La Contraviesa, Gador and the Sierra Nevada is the region of Las Alpujarras, whose remoteness and inaccessibility has provided a haven to many a fugitive. For the Moors who fled here after the fall of Granada, and the legendary bandits and Republicans who sought refuge here after the civil war, the region has played its role. It now has a growing appeal to expatriates seeking a different sort of retreat.

The cliff-top town of Ronda offers spectacular views of the ravine below and surrounding landscapes

Costa del Sol's Famous

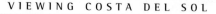

Insired by Granada
The celebrated composer Manuel de Falla lived in Granada for some 20 years, producing great works. American author Washington Irving made his own contribution in propagating the mystique of the Alhambra, with his *Tale of the Alhambra*, written during his stay here in the 1820s.

Writers, Romantics and Travellers

In the 18th and 19th centuries a number of writers, romantics and intrepid travellers discovered for themselves the attractions of Málaga and wrote about it. Hans Christian Andersen, who stayed here towards the middle of the 19th century, wrote of the joyous way of life. Lord Byron, George Borrow and Richard Ford were among others who contributed to discovering Málaga as a winter holiday destination. Later,

the interior of the region attracted writers and poets such as Rainer Maria Rilke, Gerald Brenan and Ernest Hemingway.

Art

One of Málaga's most famous sons is the celebrated painter Pablo Ruiz Picasso who was born here in 1881. He began to paint at the age of seven, later joining the School of Fine Arts in La Coruña and moving to Barcelona in 1895. A new Picasso museum is scheduled to open in Málaga in 2000.

Stars and Celebrities

By the 1960s the tourism industry had developed along the Costa del Sol and the Marbella Club, creation of Alfonso de Hohenlohe, began to attract the rich and famous. Very soon Marbella had acquired a reputation as a playground for the jet set. Since then the area has seen a flood of personalities who have come and gone, adding their mark to the star-studded scene.

Above right: Lord Byron was an early enthusiast of Málaga
Above: Málaga is justly proud of its famous son Pablo Picasso

The Field of Sport

Given its emphasis on sport, especially golf, it is not surprising that the Costa del Sol continues to receive its fair share of sports personalities. In the world of golf, Severiano Ballesteros and José Mariá Olazáble are frequent visitors. Tennis stars Bjorn Borg, Arantxa Sanchez Vicario, Conchita Martínez and Alberto Beresategui visit the area, and former champion Manolo Santana runs a tennis club at the hotel Puente Romano. The 1970s saw the founding of the Lew Hoad Campo de Tennis in Mijas by the champion, who has since died.

Top Ten

La Alcazaba, Málaga	16
La Alhambra, Granada	17
Casares	18
Cuevas de Nerja	19
La Giralda and La Catedral, Sevilla	20
Marbella's Casco Antiguo	21
La Mezquita, Córdoba	22
Mijas	23
Puerto Banús	24–5
Ronda's Puente Nuevo	26

1
La Alcazaba, Málaga

✚ 31C2

✉ Calle Alcazaba s/n

☎ 952 22 00 43

🕐 Wed–Mon 9:30–6:30.
Closed Tue. (Parts of
the building are still
closed due to
restoration works)

🍴 Many near by

🚉 Málaga railway station

♿ Few

✋ Free

ℹ Málaga (➤ 29)

*The cool patios, gardens
and fountains of La
Alcazaba offer refuge from
the heat of the town*

*The old Moorish fortress or alcazaba,
dating back to the second half of the 11th century,
stands high above the city of Málaga.*

Just up from the Plaza de Aduana are the solid, fortified
walls of La Alcazaba, landmark of Málaga. The fortress
dates back to the 700s, but most of the structure belongs
to the mid-11th century. Entrance is through the gateway
known as the Puerta del Cristo (Christ's Door), where the
first mass was celebrated following the Christian victory
over the town.

The way leads up through attractively laid out gardens
and fountains, passing through the gateways of Puerta de
las Columnas, Arco del Cristo and Arcos de Granada.
Terraces offer magnificent views of the town and harbour.
A small palace within the inner perimeter is now the home
of the Museo Arqueológico (Archaeological Museum,
➤ 37).

Just below the entrance to the Alcazaba are the ruins of
a Roman amphitheatre. Dating back to the second
century AD, they were uncovered only fairly recently and are
currently under restoration. The way above leads steeply up
to the castle which crowns the Gibralfaro Hill (➤ 32).

2
La Alhambra, Granada

One of Spain's greatest splendours, the world famous palace of La Alhambra remains as a legacy of the rich culture brought to the peninsula by the Moors.

The Alhambra holds a commanding position above the city of Granada, backed by the snowcapped peaks of the Sierra Nevada. In 1984 it joined the World Heritage list of UNESCO. Built by the Moors between the 13th and 15th centuries, it was used as a residence by Muhammad I, and members of the Nasrid dynasty.

Walk up to the entrance from the Plaza Nueva. To the east is the Renaissance palace of Emperor Carlos V, started in 1526 but never completed. To the west stands the Alcazaba, the oldest building on the site. Climb up to the top of the Vela tower for stunning views of Granada and the Sierra Nevada.

A tour of the interior of the Casa Real (Royal Palace) reveals the true marvels of the Alhambra: the beautifully decorated Patio de Mexuar, the attractive Patio de los Arrayanes (named after the myrtle trees which line a rectangular pool), and the sumptuous Salón de los Embajadores (Ambassadors' Hall) with its richly carved and coffered ceiling. The Sala de los Abencerrajes has an impressive stalactite ceiling, and the Sala de las Dos Hermanas (Hall of the Two Sisters) features a delicate honeycomb dome. The focal point is the Patio de los Leones (Courtyard of Lions) named after the 12 figures which surround the central fountain.

On the nearby Cerro del Sol (Hill of the Sun) stands the Palacio del Generalife. Dating back to the early 1300s, it was the summer palace of the Moorish kings. The gardens exude an aura of romance, with pools and fountains amidst greenery and flowers.

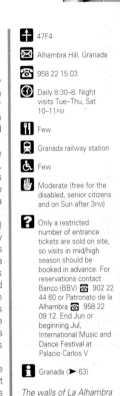

✚ 47F4

✉ Alhambra Hill, Granada

☎ 958 22 15 03

🕐 Daily 8:30–8. Night visits Tue–Thu, Sat 10–11PM

🍴 Few

🚉 Granada railway station

♿ Few

✋ Moderate (free for the disabled, senior citizens and on Sun after 3PM)

❓ Only a restricted number of entrance tickets are sold on site, so visits in mid/high season should be booked in advance. For reservations contact Banco (BBV) ☎ 902 22 44 60 or Patronato de la Alhambra ☎ 958 22 09 12. End Jun or beginning Jul, International Music and Dance Festival at Palacio Carlos V

ℹ Granada (➤ 63)

The walls of La Alhambra are bathed in the golden glow of early evening

3
Casares

✚ 46A1

✉ 105km west of Málaga

🍴 Several restaurants

🚌 Local buses

♿ Few

↔ Gaucín (► 62)

❓ August Fair (early Aug)

ℹ Tourist information:
Avenida de San
Lorenzo, Estepona
☎ 952 80 20 02

With its mass of whitewashed houses sprawling up the hillside, Casares has aquired a reputation for being the most photogenic town in Andalucía.

From whichever angle you approach, the views of Casares are spectacular. The town is easily accessible from the coast: a turning from Estepona leads up into the hills of the Sierra Bermeja. While the drive itself takes you through a scenic route of hills and wooded areas, nothing prepares you for the spectacular view of Casares with its white houses spread over the hill and crowned by an old Moorish castle. Casares saw many battles between the warring Moslems, until it was taken by the Christians in the mid 15th century.

The sight of Casares sprawling over the hillside in a cluster of white houses is always breathtaking

Much of the charm of Casares can be discovered by strolling through its white, terraced streets to the castle above. On the way up, take a look at the 17th-century church of San Sebastian, which contains a statue of the Virgen del Rosario del Campo. The fortress was built in the 13th century on Roman foundations. The 16th-century Church of the Incarnation features a Mudéjar tower.

The views become more spectacular as you make your way up to the summit, where you will be rewarded by a panorama over olive groves, orchards and forests, to the blue of the Mediterranean Sea. Take a look too at the local cemetery, which is beautifully kept and adorned with flowers – not to be missed.

4
Cuevas de Nerja

This series of caverns, close to the coastal town of Nerja, contains spectacular rock formations, and palaeolithic paintings (not open to the public).

➕ 47E2

✉ 4km east of Nerja

☎ 952 52 15 31 (i. Nerja)

🕐 Daily 10–2 and 4–6:30

🍴 Restaurant (££)

🚗 Best by car

♿ None

✋ Cheap

↔ Nerja (► 70)

❓ Summer concerts and ballet performances

ℹ Nerja (► 70)

The stunning rock formations found in the Cuevas de Nerja are a big tourist attraction

These limestone caves were discovered by chance in 1959 by a group of boys who were out and about exploring. Beyond the first grotto great caverns revealed a wonderful world of stalactites and stalagmites, some wall paintings and various items such as stone tools and fragments of pottery. Investigations by experts show that the area must have been inhabited by man over 20,000 years ago. A group of sculptures near the entrance to the caves honours the boys who made the discovery. A small archaeological museum is also located here.

The rock paintings of horses, deer, goats and dolphins are not open for public viewing, but photographs of them are on display, together with some of the artefacts found here. For the tourist, however, the attraction lies in the magnificent display of formations which are enhanced by special lighting effects.

The first chamber provides a magnificent setting for concerts which are held here as part of an annual summer festival. The next cavern is called the Hall of Ghosts after a strange shroud-like figure which appears in the stone. Most impressive, however, is the huge Hall of Cataclysms, which features a very tall column rising from a mass of stalactites.

5
La Giralda & La Catedral, Sevilla

The minaret tower known as La Giralda, seen as a symbol of Sevilla, rises proudly above the great Cathedral, third largest in Europe.

✚ 42B2

✉ Plaza Virgen de los Reyes

☎ 954 21 49 71

🕐 Mon–Sat 11–5, Sun 2–6

🍴 Many restaurants near by

🚉 RENFE station

♿ Few

✋ Moderate; Sun free

ℹ Sevilla (➤ 81)

The 98m-high brick tower of La Giralda is a prominent feature of Sevilla. It was built in the 12th century as the minaret of the former Great Mosque. In 1565 a section with 25 bells was added and topped with a bronze statue representing Faith, which acts as a *giralda* (weather vane). There are good views of the town from the first gallery.

The cathedral, which was built in the Gothic style, with some Renaissance influences, is very grand. The interior is awe-inspiring for its sheer size and the richness of its decoration, with solid Gothic columns supporting massive arches which reach up to the great heights of the vaulted ceiling.

Three attractive Plateresque grilles in the Sanctuary hide an immense golden Gothic altarpiece which rates as one of the cathedral's greatest glories and is said to be the largest altar in the world. Started by the Flemish artist Dancart in 1482, it took almost a hundred years to complete the 45 tableaux depicting the life of Jesus and Mary. Above the 16th-century shrine stands an image of the Virgen de la Sede.

The choirstalls are fine examples of flamboyant Gothic. Notable also is the Capilla Real (Royal Chapel). Completed in 1575, it features a richly decorated Renaissance cupola. On either side are the tombs of King Alfonso X (the Wise) and his mother, Beatrice of Swabia. In the south transept lies the ornate tomb of Christopher Columbus, whose body lay here for a time after it was transported from Cuba.

Above: *the Giralda tower is a symbol of Sevilla*

Right: *Sevilla's great Gothic cathedral has a rich interior*

6
Marbella's Casco Antiguo

The jewel of Marbella is its Casco Antiguo (Old Town), a picturesque maze of narrow streets, pretty squares and whitewashed houses.

Located to the north of Avenida Ramón y Cajal, which cuts through the town, Marbella's old quarter is a delightful area in which to browse with its flower-filled streets, neat little houses and small squares. Among its prettiest streets are Remedios, Dolores, Rincón de la Virgen and San Cristóbal which are noted for the brilliance of their flower displays.

Sooner or later everyone converges on the Plaza de los Naranjos, a charming little square lined with neatly pruned orange trees. This is a popular place for a drink or meal out in the open where you can enjoy its lively atmosphere. In the middle of the square is a bust of a serene-looking King Juan Carlos.

42C1

Marbella (56km west of Málaga)

Many restaurants (£–£££)

Marbella bus stop, Avenida Ricardo Soriano 21 (Bus station Calle Trapiche ☎ 952 76 44 00)

Few

Remnants of city walls

Pre-Lent Carnival; Feria de San Bernabé (11–18 Jun)

Evidence of its Moorish, Christian and Roman past can be seen on many of its buildings. Take a look at the Iglesia de la Incarnación and, above it, the remaining towers of an old Moorish fortress; the 16th-century Ayuntamiento (Town Hall), Casa Consistorial, which boasts a fine Mudéjar entrance and the Ermita de Nuestro Señor Santiago, Marbella's earliest Christian church. Worth a glimpse, too, is the attractive little Cofradía del Santo Christo de Amor chapel, situated at one end of the Plaza de los Naranjos. A stroll through this area is particularly enjoyable in spring when the heady scent of orange blossom fills the air.

Calle San Cristóbal is one of the enchanting little streets which form the heart of Marbella's old town

21

7
La Mezquita, Córdoba

42C3

Torrijos y Cardenal Herrero

957 47 05 12

Mon–Sat 10–7, Sun 2–7

Many restaurants near by (£–£££)

RENFE station, Avenida de America, Córdoba

Few

Moderate

Córdoba (➤ 51)

The great mosque of Córdoba is a unique monument which stands as a remarkable achievement of Moorish architecture.

The Mezquita of Córdoba was built in four stages between the 8th and 10th centuries and features amongst the world's largest mosques, remaining as a testimony to the immense power of Islam at the height of its domination of the peninsula.

Do not be discouraged by the mosque's somewhat forbidding outward appearance: its beauty lies within. The main entrance is through the Puerta del Perdón, which leads into the Patio de los Naranjos (Courtyard of the Oranges). Once inside you will be confronted by myriad columns of onyx, marble and granite. The light effects within this dim interior are sensational. The columns are topped by decorated capitals and crowned by the striking red and white arches so characteristic of Moorish architecture. There is a sense of awe and mysticism, special to this particular mosque, which lures the visitor back time and time again.

The striking Moorish interior of Córdoba's fabled mosque is seen as one of Andalucía's richest jewels

To find a Christian cathedral within the very heart of the mosque comes as something of a surprise. It was built in the 1520s on the orders of Hapsburg Emperor Carlos V, who later regretted his decision. However, it does manage to blend fairly well into its surroundings.

Rising above the Puerta del Perdón is the bell tower, which offers splendid views.

8

Mijas

With its attractive mountain setting, picturesque little streets and whitewashed houses, Mijas is a popular excursion from the coast.

Despite the fact that Mijas caters so obviously for the tourist it has still managed to retain its charm. The little town is undeniably picturesque, with its white houses, narrow winding streets, flowers and plants. The setting is most attractive, offering magnificent views of the pine-clad mountains which surround it and the coast below. Furthermore, its proximity to the coast, a drive of some 20 minutes or so, makes it an ideal destination for a day's excursion.

On the central square of Plaza de la Virgen you will see the ever-patient donkeys lined up. Adorned with colourful saddles and tassles, they can be hired for rides around town, serving as donkey taxis. Concerts and fiestas are sometimes held in the square, which centres around a small fountain and is a popular meeting place. Below is a large parking lot, which has greatly helped to ease traffic problems.

Adjoining the square is a neat little park which offers magnificent views all around. Hollowed out from a chunk of rock is a delightful little chapel known as the Santuario de la Virgen de la Peña Limosnas. Inside is the image of Santa Maria de la Peña, along with some impressive candlesticks, embroidered garments and other religious relics.

On the Plaza de la Constitución stands the Iglesia de la Concepción, which was built in the 17th century, mostly in the Mozarabe style. Near by is the town's small bullring. The author Ronald Fraser wrote two books about Mijas: *The Pueblo* and *In Hiding*.

The picturesque little mountain town of Mijas

46C2

37km west of Málaga

Many restaurants (£–£££)

Local bus services

Few

Benalmádena Pueblo (► 47)

St Anthony's Day (16–17 Jan); Fería de la Virgen de la Peña (early Sep); Romería de Santa Teresa (end Oct)

Tourist information: Ayuntamiento, Plaza de la Peña ☎ 952 48 59 00

9
Puerto Banús

 46B1

 64km west of Málaga, 6km west of Marbella town

Many bars and restaurants (££–£££)

Bus stop Hotel Andalucía Plaza

 Few

 San Pedro de Alcántara (► 78)

Regattas, sailing and fishing competitions

Tourist Information: Avenida Principal s/n ☎ 952 81 74 74 (summer only)

The dazzling marina of Puerto Banús, with its luxurious yachts, trendy restaurants and bars, serves as a magnet for visitors to the Costa del Sol.

A stay on the Costa del Sol would be incomplete without a visit to Puerto Banús, one of the Costa's most famous attractions. Built in 1968, Puerto José Banús, as it is also known, was the creation of promoter José Banús and was one of Spain's first village-type harbour developments. The result is most attractive and worth a visit.

Backed by the mountains, a ring of brilliant white apartment houses surrounds the marina, which is filled with craft of all sizes, from mega yachts to small sailing

Above: *enjoying a drink in lively Banús*

Right: *the yacht-filled harbour of Puerto Banús presents a glamorous scene*

boats. A feature of Banús is the Arab-built complex of luxury apartments, located on the right as you enter the port. With its opulent marble façade and gleaming turrets, the inspiration could have been taken straight from the *Arabian Nights*.

Around the port is a string of cafés, bars and restaurants, along with boutiques and gift shops. While frontline restaurants are *the* places in which to be seen, better value is sometimes found in some of the small restaurants in the streets behind, tucked away up flights of stairs. In season the quayside is thronged with people who come to see, or to be seen – this can be a great place for celebrity-spotting.

At night the place becomes a hive of activity, as the smart restaurants, trendy piano bars, discos and nightclubs fill up with beautiful people. The tastefully done Benabola development is a good spot for watching the sunset over a drink, in more relaxed surroundings.

10
Ronda's Puente Nuevo

➕ 46A2

✉️ 118km northwest of Málaga

🍽️ Many restaurants in Ronda (£–£££)

🚌 Buses from Algeciras, Málaga (via Bobadilla)

↔️ Ronda (➤ 74), Cuevas de la Pileta (➤ 75)

ℹ️ Ronda (➤ 74)

The old town of Ronda is famed for its spectacular setting and views of the bridge over the El Tajo ravine.

Ronda has long associations with painters and writers, for many of whom the town has held a deep fascination. The scene of Ronda perched on the clifftop and, in particular, the bridge which spans the gorge, has been the subject of countless paintings and photographs.

Ronda is one of Spain's oldest cities. Situated within the rugged landscape of the Serranía de Ronda, the town is split in two, divided by the gorge of the River Guadalevín, which is spanned by the Puente Nuevo (New Bridge). The dramatic views from the bridge, combined with the attractions of the old town and its historical interest, make Ronda (➤ 74) a top excursion for visitors staying along the coast.

The Puente Nuevo (which has become the city's symbol) was begun in 1751 and completed in 1793. It stands a full 96m above the Tajo gorge at its highest and narrowest point. The unfortunate architect fell to his death from a basket lowered to allow him to inspect the building work.

The Puente Nuevo spans the deep Tajo gorge, linking the old Ronda with the 'new town'

What
To See

Málaga   28–39
Costa del Sol and Beyond 40–90
In the Know   54–5
Food and Drink   72–3

Málaga

Málaga is the second city of Andalucía and capital of the Costa del Sol, forming a natural divide between its western and eastern sections. The town has an attractive setting, crowned by the old Moorish castle which stands atop the Gibralfaro Hill, holding a commanding view of Málaga's harbour and the wide sweep of the bay.

The backing of the Montes de Málaga mountain range provides shelter from the wind, ensuring a pleasant Mediterranean climate which is particularly agreeable from autumn through to spring.

These days, however, since mass tourism took off along the coast, Málaga has tended to serve primarily as a gateway to the region. It has a lot more to offer than meets the eye, however. Exploring its old haunts and churches, sampling the local bars and restaurants will bring you home to something of the real flavour of Andalucía.

'The people all looked in a good humour... They gave me a feeling of joy and exhilaration. O Málaga, glorious city, here shall I be at home!'

HANS CHRISTAIN ANDERSEN
A Visit to Spain (1862)

Málaga

Málaga has, by and large, retained its own personality over the years, remaining relatively untouched by the tourist boom along the coast. In the early 19th century Málaga found favour with the British who started coming here to take advantage of its mild Mediterranean winters. The town later suffered a long period of decline but is now enjoying a revival.

It is well worth spending some time to explore the town. Off the Alameda Principal, Málaga's main avenue, attractively shaded by palms and lined with flower stalls and kiosks, is the old town. Here you will find yourself in another world of narrow streets with traditional bars and *bodegas* exuding a decidedly local flavour.

Major sights include the cathedral, a number of churches each with its own distinctive style and a few museums. This is all contained within a small area and can easily be covered on foot. A highlight is a visit to the Alcazaba (▶ 16) and Castillo de Gibralfaro (▶ 32), which offer magnificent views of the town and bay. For good seafood restaurants head for the beach suburbs of El Palo or Pedregalejo, east of the town.

A good way to visit the town is by the electric train which runs half hourly between Fuengirola and Málaga, making stops at Torremolinos and other centres en route.

The Gibralfaro castle offers a panoramic view of Málaga town, with the harbour and coastline beyond

🛈 Tourist information:
Pasaje de Chinitas 4
☎ 952 21 34 45

29

🚹 31C2
✉ Plaza de la Merced 15
☎ 952 06 02 15
🕐 Mon–Sat 1–2, 5–8; Sun 11–2
🍴 Many near by (£–£££)
🚉 RENFE station Centro-Alameda
♿ Few
🖐 Free

What to See in Málaga

CASA NATAL DE PICASSO ⭐

Spain's celebrated painter, Pablo Ruiz Picasso, was born in 1881 in the corner house of an elegant yellow-toned block on Plaza de la Merced. His birthplace was declared an historic-artistic monument in 1983, and in 1991 it became the headquarters of the Pablo Ruiz Picasso Foundation. The centre has been created to foster cultural activities, including the promotion of contemporary art with a special emphasis on Picasso himself.

Visitors are welcome to take a look around the small area on the first floor where you can see a few photographs, memorabilia and documentation relating to Picasso's life, in addition to works by other artists.

It was here that Picasso began to paint, helped by his father, an art teacher, who had recognised his young son's talent.

Picasso Museum
A new Picasso Museum is being installed in the Palacio Buenavista, former home of the Palace of Fine Arts. Scheduled to open on 28 February 2000, the museum will contain over 180 works by the artist, including drawings, engravings, lithographs, sculptures and ceramics donated by Picasso's daughter-in-law Christina. For further information contact Delegacón de Cultura ☎ 952 21 36 40, or your local tourist office.

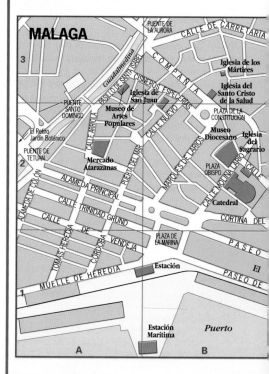

The site of Málaga's Gibralfaro castle was once occupied by a lighthouse which served to guide the ships into the harbour

The energetic can take a walk up the Gibralfaro Hill to the castle, which stands above the Alcazaba

32

➕ 31D1
✉ Lighthouse Hill
☎ 952 22 00 43
🕐 Daily 9:30–6
🍴 Parador near by
♿ None
🎫 Free

CASTILLO DE GIBRALFARO ⭐

Right above the Alcazaba stands the Castillo de Gibralfaro, crowning the hill of the same name. It was built by Yusef I of Granada at the beginning of the 14th century on a formerly Phoenician site and lighthouse from which its name was derived – *gebel-faro* (rock of the lighthouse) signifies the beacon that served to guide ships into the harbour.

This was once the scene of a three-month siege by the citizens of Málaga against the Catholic monarchs Ferdinand and Isabella. The matter was concluded only when hunger led to capitulation, after which Ferdinand occupied the site while his queen took up residence in the town. All that remains today of this historic monument is a series of solid ramparts which rise majestically among dense woods of pines and eucalyptus, with the Alcazaba not far below.

It can be reached on foot, by means of a fairly arduous walk up the hill by the Alcazaba. Alternatively you could get there by horse and carriage or taxi. You can always round off with a cool drink at the nearby Parador Málaga-Gibralfaro, which also offers panoramic views of the city and harbour, with landmarks such as the cathedral and bullring clearly visible.

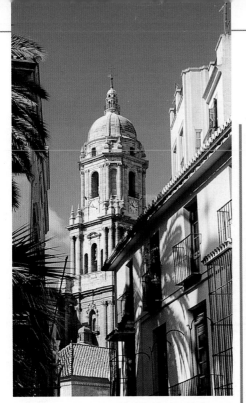

Left: *the solitary steeple of Málaga's cathedral*

Below: *fine carving on the choir stalls in the cathedral*

CATEDRAL ★

Málaga's cathedral is large and has a somewhat sombre exterior. It was built between 1528 and 1782 on or near the site of a former mosque. While original plans had allowed for two towers, lack of funds resulted in the completion of only one, giving rise to the name by which the cathedral is affectionately referred to, La Manquita, loosely interpreted as 'the little one-armed woman'.

The interior has influences of the Renaissance and baroque styles. The notable 17th-century choir stalls of mahogany and cedarwood were designed by Luis Ortiz. After his death the 40 finely carved statues of the saints behind each stall were completed by Pedro de Mena, one of Spain's most celebrated wood-carvers of the time, who spent some years in Málaga. Some of the chapels leading off the aisles also contain works by Pedro de Mena and his tutor Alonso Cano.

Adjoining the cathedral is the Iglesia del Sagrario. Founded in the 15th century on the site of a mosque, the church has an unusual rectangular shape. Its Isabelline-Gothic portal is the only remaining part of the original structure, which was rebuilt in 1714. The interior is richly decorated and its main altar features a magnificent 16th-century retable.

✚ 30B2
✉ Calle Molina Lario
☎ 952 21 59 17
🕐 Mon–Sat 9–6:45. Closed Sun
🍴 None
🚉 RENFE station Centro-Alameda
♿ Few
💷 Cheap

+ 30A2
🍴 Huge choice of
restaurants (£–£££)

*Above: Málaga's harbour
bustling with activity*

*Below: Málaga's old
narrow streets can lead
to many a surprise*

CENTRO (CENTRE) ⭐

The heart of Málaga is found north of the Alameda
Principal, Málaga's main avenue, and east of the Río
Guadalmedina, which separates the old town from the
new. As soon as you turn off the Alameda you will enter a
labyrinthine mediaeval world of narrow, twisting roads.
There is much to be enjoyed here, increasingly so the
more you find your bearings. The centre is small and many
streets are pedestrianised, so that exploring on foot is both
enjoyable and viable.

Another way in which to enjoy a little tour around town
is by horse-drawn carriage, a good option if you are tired or
feeling the heat. You will see these lined up by the
cathedral, in the Paseo del Parque and various other points
around the town.

While the cathedral is a focal point from which to start
exploring, the main artery of the city centre is the busy
shopping street, Calle Marqués de Larios, which leads
from the Alameda Principal north to the Plaza de la
Constitución. On either side are old, narrow streets,
alleyways and tiny squares where you can happily browse
for hours. Within this area are a number of churches and a
few museums, all within close range. You will also
discover some delightfully picturesque little streets lined
with gaily coloured houses and shops.

Málaga is famed for its *tapas* bars. For some local
atmosphere try one of the so-called *rutas del tapeo* (*tapas*
route) which cover the area west of Calle Marqués de
Larios, centering around Calle Nueva.

A Walk Through the Old Town

This walk starts in the Plaza de la Marina and makes a tour of Málaga's old quarters, taking in the cathedral and several churches.

From Plaza de la Marina take Calle Molina Lario, left of the Málaga Palace Hotel which faces you. A few moments' walk will bring you right up to the cathedral.

Horses and carriages line up here ready to take visitors on a tour around the town. Opposite, on the Plaza Obispo, is the old Palacio Episcopal, which now houses exhibitions of contemporary art.

Proceed along Calle Agustín.

You will pass on your right the Palacio Buenavista. Formerly the home of the Museo de Bellas Artes, this is now being converted into the new Museo Picasso. You will now enter an attractive section of pedestrianised streets and pretty coloured houses.

Take a right fork into Calle Granada which takes you by the Iglesia de Santiago. From here continue to the Plaza de la Merced.

The centre of the Plaza de la Merced is marked by an obelisk in memory of General Torrijos and his men who were shot after the War of Independence. On the far corner, in an attractive block of houses, is the Casa Natal de Picasso, birthplace of Pablo Picasso, now centre of the Picasso Foundation.

Return down Calle Granada to Plaza del Siglo and on to the Plaza de la Constitucíon, then stroll down Calle Marqués Larios, Málaga's main shopping street. Down on the left make a short detour through the archway and along Pasaje de Chinitas, which leads to a tiny square. Complete the walk down Calle Larios and turn into the Alameda Principal to Plaza de la Marina.

The statue of Santa Maria de la Victoria is one of many sculptures to be seen at Málaga's cathedral

Distance
4km

Time
3–4 hours, depending on visits to churches

Start/end point
Plaza de la Marina
✚ 30B1

Lunch
Espartero (££)
✉ Espartero 4
☎ 952 60 30 22

The Iglesia de los Mártires
(Church of the Martyrs)
has a fine Mudéjar tower

Iglesias (Churches)

When strolling about Málaga's old town, you are more than likely to pass by several, if not all, of the following churches. Take time to have a look inside, as each has its own individual attraction. With the exception of the Santuario de la Victoria, which is slightly away from the centre, all are within easy walking distance of each other.

CATEDRAL (► 33)

IGLESIA DE LOS MÁRTIRES

The church was founded in 1487 by the Catholic Kings and dedicated to the martyrs of the town. It features a striking Mudéjar tower which was added later and a richly decorated baroque-style interior, which includes a notable sculpture by Francisco Ortíz of Jesus praying on the Mount of Olives.

IGLESIA DE SANTIAGO

Founded in 1490, the church is noted for its tall, Mudéjar-style steeple and baroque interior which contains some notable chapels. Pablo Picasso's baptismal certificate is stored here.

IGLESIA DEL SANTO CRISTO DE LA SALUD

The interior of this 17th-century church is a real gem. Note the brilliant altarpiece and beautifully decorated cupola. The church also contains the tomb of architect Pedro de la Mena.

IGLESIA SAN JUAN BAUTISTA

Founded in 1490, the church's baroque-style tower above the main entrance was added in 1770. Inside are several fine chapels and a rich altarpiece. The 17th-century figure of San Juan is the work of Francisco Ortíz.

SANTUARIO DE LA VICTORIA

The church was erected in 1487 on the site where the Catholic Monarchs pitched their tents during the siege of that year. Its main feature is the magnificent retable which rises above the main altar. High up, amidst a flourish of exuberant ornamentation, is a small camerín (chapel) containing a statue of the Madonna and Child. In the crypt below is the family vault of the counts of Buenavista, who were responsible for the rebuilding of the church in the 17th century.

30B3
Plaza Mártires
952 21 27 24
Open daily 8–1 and 7–8
Few
Free

31C2
Calle Granada 62
952 21 03 99
Open daily 9–1:30 and 6–8

30B3
Calle Compania
952 21 34 56

30B3
Calle San Juan
952 21 12 83
Open daily 8:30–1, 6–8

Off map 31D2
Plaza del Santuario
952 25 26 47
Open Tue–Sun 8–1 and 4–8
Centro-Alameda railway station
Few
Free

MUSEO DE ARTES Y COSTUMBRES POPULARES ✪✪

This charming little museum is housed in the Mesón de la Victoria, a former 17th-century inn, now attractively restored. The museum is on two floors and was created to give an insight into the past ways and customs of the people of the region.

The first rooms, which display agricultural items, open out onto an attractive courtyard with tropical plants. In the rooms beyond you can see a fishing boat and some

➕ 30A3
✉ Passillo de Santa Isabel 10
☎ 952 21 71 37
🕐 Tue–Fri 10–1:30, 4–7. Closed Sat afternoon and Sun
🚉 Railway station Centro-Alameda
♿ Few 💰 Cheap

interiors of old houses. Upstairs displays include collections of costumes, ceramics and tiles, fascinating old posters announcing fiestas, religious items and an enchanting little group of clay figures depicting a *panda de verdiales* (group of regional musicians).

Above: leafy courtyard of the Museo de Artes Populares

MUSEO ARQUEOLÓGICO ✪✪✪

Within the main palace of the Alcazaba (➤ 16) is the Museo Arqueológico (Archaeological Museum) which is contained within a series of courtyards with Moorish decoration and has a room with a fine Mudéjar ceiling. There are exhibits from the prehistoric, Phoenician, Roman and Moorish times, plus ceramics, glassware, coins and Alcazaba models. The terrace offers good views over the city and harbour.

➕ 31C2
✉ Calle Alcazaba, s/n
🕐 Wed–Mon 9:30–6:30. Closed Tue
♿ Few
💰 Cheap

Left: one of the Museo de Artes Populares' old 'Grandes Fiestas' posters

Parques y Jardines (Parks & Gardens)

In and around Málaga are several attractive parks and gardens, of which the following are outstanding.

EL PARQUE

Malaga's city park, which runs alongside the Paseo del Parque, was created at the end of the 19th century making use of land reclaimed from the sea. The park contains beautiful tropical flowering trees and shrubs. Many of the unusual and exotic species to be seen here were brought from overseas when Málaga was an important world trading centre.

EL RETIRO JARDÍN BOTÁNICO-ORNITOLÓGICO

The El Retiro Park is an old botanic garden and bird sanctuary, where monks once came to find peace and to meditate. Recently opened to the public, its ornithological park contains hundreds of birds, many of them endangered species. A peaceful stroll can be enjoyed amongst its trees, ponds and fountains.

JARDÍN BOTÁNICO-HISTÓRICO 'LA CONCEPCIÓN'

Just outside Málaga, Finca de la Concepción is another magnificent botanic garden. You can follow a marked path through exotic trees and plants, passing Roman sculpture and a waterfall.

30B1/31C1
Between Paseo del Parque and Paseo de Espana
None
Daily
Good
Free

Off map 30A2
Ctra de Coin
952 62 16 00
Daily 9–6
Restaurant (££)
Few
Moderate

46C2
Along the N331 to Antequera, just off the Málaga ring road
952 25 21 48
Tue–Sun 10–4:30. Closed Mon
Few
Cheap

The Paseo del Parque offers a delightful stroll amidst shady trees, fountains and colourful tropical plants

A Walk Around the Churches & Museums of Málaga

This is a leisurely walk which includes Málaga's main market, an attractive little museum and several churches.

From the Centro–Alameda take the Alameda Principal exit. Cross over at the traffic lights and turn into Calle Torregarda to the Mercado de Atarazas, Malaga's main market.

Pass through the market to take a look at the colourful displays of fruit and vegetables and, in particular, the wonderful selection of glistening fresh fish.

Emerge into Calle Arriola and take the Paseo Santa Isabel.

You will find yourself on the banks of the dried up Río Guadalmedina. Look out for a flight of steps on your right which leads down through a tiny garden to the Museo de Artes Populares.

Continue along the Paseo Santa Isabel and turn right down Calle Cisneros.

This brings you into a picturesque part of the old town where a right turn down a narrow alleyway leads to the Iglesia San Juan, standing on a small square.

Retrace your steps, turn right, then left along Calle Salvago to Plaza San Ignacio.

Take a look at the Iglesia del Corazón de Jesús. Turn back and take the Calle de los Mártires. On the small square which follows you cannot miss the striking Mudéjar tower of the Iglesia de los Mártires.

Return and turn left along Calle Compañia, which leads past the Iglesia de Santo Cristo de la Salud.

Wander through the Plaza de la Constitución and take the Calle Nueva into the heart of Malaga's famous area for *tapas* bars. Some refreshments will no doubt be welcome here. The Calle Puerta del Mar leads straight down to the Alameda Principal and back to the station.

Distance
3.5km

Time
3–4 hours, depending on visits

Start/end point
Railway station Centro-Alameda
✠ 30B1

Lunch
La Manchega (££)
✉ Marín García
☎ 952 22 21 80

A stroll in the old quarters of the town will take you by some colourful old façades

Costa del Sol & Beyond

The Costa del Sol falls into two parts with Málaga forming the divide between the western and eastern sections. The most developed and best known area starts west of Málaga and includes the major resorts of Torremolinos, Fuengirola, Marbella and Estepona. This part of the coastline is virtually one long stream of apartment blocks, developments, hotels and restaurants, with an increasing number of marinas.

The eastern Costa del Sol, stretching towards Almería, has a totally different appeal. The coastline is often broken up by rocks and small coves and is much less developed, with Nerja standing out as a favoured resort.

The interior offers countless excursions to delightful white Andalucían villages nestling in the mountains, and to the great historic cities of Granada, Córdoba and Sevilla.

*'The road to Málaga followed a
beautiful but exhausted shore,
seemingly forgotten by the world.
I remember the names –
San Pedro, Estepona, Marbella
and FuengirolaÑ'*

LAURIE LEE
*As I Walked Out One Midsummer
Morning* 1969

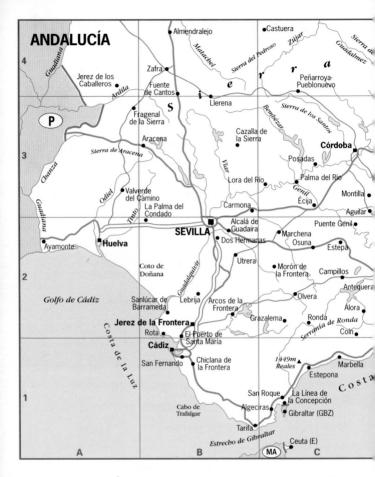

ANDALUCÍA

(map labels)

Almendralejo • Castuera

Matachel

Sierra del Pedroso · Zújar

Sierra de Guadalmez

Jerez de los Caballeros

Zafra

Fuente de Cantos

Peñarroya-Pueblonuevo

Ardila

Llerena

Sierra de los Santos

Fragenal de la Sierra

Aracena

Cazalla de la Sierra

Córdoba

Sierra de Aracena

Posadas

Viar

Palma del Río

Montilla

Valverde del Camino

Lora del Río

Écija

Aguilar

La Palma del Condado

Carmona

Alcalá de Guadaira

Puente Genil

SEVILLA

Marchena

Osuna

Estepa

Ayamonte

Huelva

Dos Hermanas

Utrera

Morón de la Frontera

Campillos

Antequera

Golfo de Cádiz

Coto de Doñana

Sanlúcar de Barrameda

Lebrija

Arcos de la Frontera

Olvera

Álora

Jerez de la Frontera

Grazalema

Ronda

Coín

Rota

El Puerto de Santa María

Serranía de Ronda

Cádiz

San Fernando

Chiclana de la Frontera

1,449m Reales

Marbella

Estepona

Costa

Cabo de Trafalgar

San Roque

La Línea de la Concepción

Algeciras

Gibraltar (GBZ)

Tarifa

Estrecho de Gibraltar

Ceuta (E)

ALMUÑECAR ●●

47F2

84km east of Málaga

Variety of restaurants

Local bus services

Few

Tourist Information: Avenida Europa-Palacete La Najarra

☎ 952 63 11 25

Almuñecar, situated in the province of Granada, within the coastline now designated as the Costa Tropical, lies amidst orchards of tropical fruits. It presents a very picturesque scene, typical of so many villages to be found in southern Spain, with a cluster of whitewashed houses rising up the hillside, crowned by an old castle. Its history goes back to the time of the Phoenicians, with subsequent occupation by the Romans and the Moors.

The Castillo de San Miguel stands on top of a tall rock, dividing two bays. It was built during the reign of Carlos V, over the site of a former Moorish fortress, and features a great square tower known as La Mazmorra.

The town itself is a delightful jumble of narrow, cobble-stoned streets, climbing steeply up to the summit. Do not

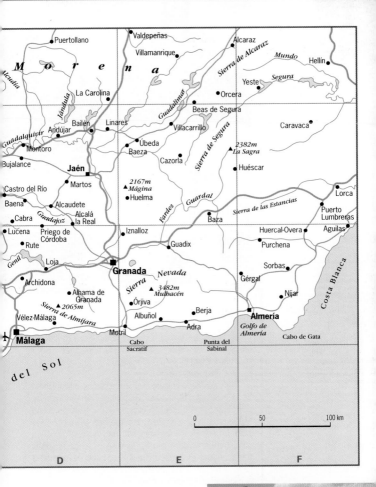

miss a visit to the Ornithological Park located at the foot of the hill. Here you can see brilliantly coloured parrots and rare species of birds in a beautiful setting of subtropical plants and flowers. The seafront is lined with apartment blocks, bars and restaurants, with a lively scene by day and night, during the season.

Also worth a visit is the small archaeological museum housed in the Cueva de los Siete Palacios, thought to have been a Roman reservoir for water. The museum has a display of artefacts from the area (open Tue–Sat 11–2 and 6–8).

A look-out post at nearby Punta de la Mona offers sweeping views of the harbour and the Mediterranean.

Almuñecar is one of the most prominent resort towns along the coast east of Málaga

43

Well worth a visit is Antequera, an interesting old town with many churches, convents and squares

 46C3
 54km north of Málaga
Good choice of restaurants (£–£££)
From Málaga
From Málaga
Few
Fería de Primavera (31 May–1/2 Jun); Noche Flamenca de Santa Maria (end Jul); August Fair (early Aug)
 Tourist Information: Plaza San Sebastian 7 ☎ 952 70 25 05

Cueva de Menga
1km east of Antequera
Daily 10–2, Tue–Fri 10–2 and 3–5:30
From Antequera
From Antequera
None
 Free

ANTEQUERA ⭐⭐
(Town Walk ➤ 45 and Drive from Torremolinos ➤ 90.)
Antequera is a town of convents, churches and elegant mansions, which show various architectural influences. It is easily reached by means of the good motorway from the coast and certainly merits a visit.

The town is dominated by the old castle, which offers good views of the surrounding plains. The 16th-century church of Santa María la Mayor, near by, features a fine Mudéjar ceiling. Dominant are the bell towers of the churches of San Sebastian and San Augustín, which combine the Mudéjar and baroque styles. Outstanding is the church of El Carmen, which has been designated a national monument. Formerly a convent, it is noted for its rich interior and impressive wooden altar.

The discovery of prehistoric tombs in nearby caves has given the town added importance. Of the three caves here, the most important is the **Cueva de Menga**. Its large cavern contains a series of stones and columns which support huge slabs that form the roof, believed to date back to circa 2500 BC.

The Parque Nacional El Torcal de Antequera is located some 16km south of Antequera and covers an extended area of grey limestone rocks and boulders which have been weathered with time to form the most weird and wonderful shapes. There is a small information office by the parking lot and a magnificent view from the nearby Mirador el Ventanillo. Several walking trails among the boulders are marked by arrows (yellow for a shorter walk, red for a longer one).

A Stroll Around Antequera's Churches & Mansions

The walk starts in the Plaza San Sebastian and takes in some of Antequera's lovely churches and elegant mansions, the Alcazaba and main centre.

On the Plaza San Sebastian take a look at the 16th-century Colegiata de San Sebastian. Walk up the busy Calle Infante Don Fernando. Take a look at the Iglesia de San Agustín, on the left, and further along, on the right, you will pass the Palacio Consistorial (Town Hall), and the Convento de los Remedios. On the other side of the road is the house of the Pardo family.

Just past the Iglesia de San Juan de Dios turn sharp right into Calle Cantareros and back towards the centre.

On your way you will pass the house of the Condado de Colchado and the Convento de la Madre de Dios de Monteagudo.

Continue along Calle Diego Ponce to the Plaza San Francisco.

Here you will see one of Antequera's National Monuments, the Convento Real de San Zoilo.

Continue down Calle Calzada through to Plaza del Carmen, which is dominated by the fine church Iglesia del Carmen. From here make your way to Calle del Colegio and pass through the Arco de los Gigantes (Arch of Giants).

Nearby are the Real Colegiata de Santa María la Mayor and the Baños Romanos (Roman Baths).

From the Arch take Calle Herradores to the charming Plaza del Portichuelo on which stands the Iglesia de Santa María de Jesús.

Distance
4.5km

Time
About 3 hours

Start point
Plaza San Sebastian
✚ 46C3

End point
Plaza del Portichuelo
✚ 46C3

Lunch
Restaurante El Angelote (££)
✉ Calle Encarnación
(Esquina Cosa Viejo)
☎ 952 70 34 65

Antequera's rooftops seen through the castle's archway

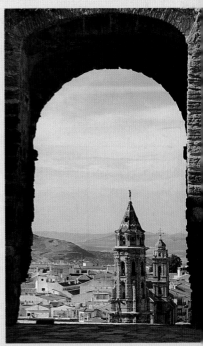

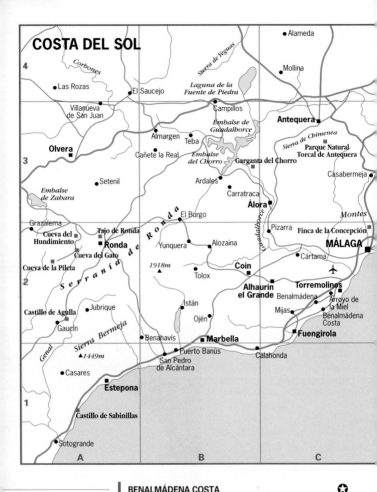

COSTA DEL SOL

(map showing locations including:)

Alameda, Mollina, Sierra de Yeguas, Corbones, Las Rozas, El Saucejo, Laguna de la Fuente de Piedra, Campillos, Antequera, Villanueva de San Juan, Embalse de Guadalhorce, Almargen, Teba, Sierra de Chimenea, Parque Natural Torcal de Antequera, Olvera, Cañete la Real, Embalse del Chorro, Garganta del Chorro, Casabermeja, Setenil, Ardales, Carratraca, Álora, Montes, Embalse de Zahara, El Burgo, Pizarra, Finca de la Concepción, MÁLAGA, Grazalema, Cueva del Hundimiento, Tajo de Ronda, Ronda, Yunquera, Alozaina, Cártama, Cueva del Gato, Serrania de Ronda, 1918m, Tolox, Coín, Cueva de la Pileta, Alhaurín el Grande, Benalmádena, Torremolinos, Istán, Mijas, Arroyo de la Miel, Castillo de Agñila, Jubrique, Ojén, Benalmádena Costa, Gaucín, Sierra Bermeja, Benahavís, Marbella, Fuengirola, Genal, 1449m, Puerto Banús, San Pedro de Alcántara, Calahonda, Casares, Estepona, Castillo de Sabinillas, Sotogrande

---

46C2

20km west of Málaga

Numerous restaurants and bars (£–£££)

Connections

Railway station Benalmádena–Arroyo de la Miel

Few

Sea Life Centre (➤ 106)

Virgen del Carmen fiesta (16 Jul)

Carretera de Cádiz 220km ☎ 952 35 00 61

BENALMÁDENA COSTA   ✪

Benalmádena Costa is, in effect, a natural extension of Torremolinos, taking over where Torremolinos leaves off. It covers a long stretch of coast lined with the type of high-rise apartment blocks which characterise this section of the Costa del Sol, along with a string of restaurants, cafés, bars and shops. An attractive seafront promenade makes it possible to walk from Torremolinos all the way along the coast to Benalmádena's Puerto Marina (➤ 48) – you need time and energy for this!

The area is being noticeably upgraded, with a new casino and the 18-hole Torrequebrada golf course, located a short distance up into the hills. There are also facilities for waterskiing, jetskiing, windsurfing, sailing and all the popular watersports.

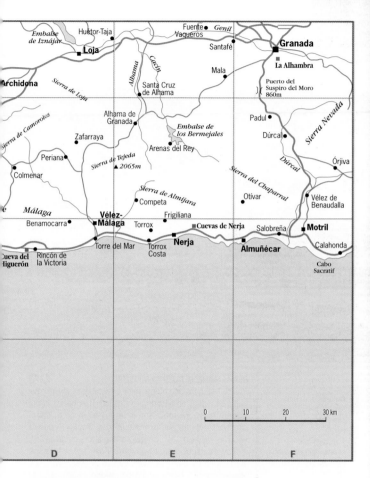

D   **E**   **F**

0   10   20   30 km

BENALMÁDENA PUEBLO ⭐⭐

Two small inland communities present a complete contrast to the attractions on the coastal strip of Benalmádena Costa. About 1km into the hills is Arroyo de la Miel which has developed into quite a lively centre with modern housing, shops and restaurants. Just up the road is the Tivoli World Show and Amusement Park.

Further up the hill is Benalmádena Pueblo whose origins are thought to date back to Phoenician times. This is a charming little village of narrow twisting streets and whitewashed houses. With attractive views of the coast and surrounding landscapes, it offers a rural atmosphere. The Museo Arqueológico contains some pre-Columbian exhibits, along with artefacts from Roman and early Iberian times.

➕ 46C2

✉ 3km west of Arroyo de la Miel

🍴 Variety of restaurants and bars

♿ Few

↔ Castillo de Aguílas (Birds of Prey Centre), Tivoli World Amusement Park (► 106)

❓ Local fair (15 Aug); Fería de San Juan (24 Jun) at Arroyo de la Miel

47

 46C2
✉ Benalmádena Costa
🍴 Variety of restaurants,
bars and pubs
 Few
↔ Torrequebrada
development with casino,
nightclub and golf course
(► 108)

*Benalmádena's fast
developing marina offers
a variety of attractions to
suit visitors of all ages*

48

BENALMÁDENA PUERTO MARINA

Puerto Marina is one of the many new marinas which have been springing up all along the coast. The marina is not evident from the road, so when driving in (from either direction) look closely for the turning to Puerto Deportivo which is easy to miss. There is parking at the entrance.

The development is fairly small and has a harbour, surrounded by a ring of whitewashed houses, giving the appearance of a typical Andalucían village. Shops, open air bars and restaurants line the quaysides. A centrepiece is provided by a complex of luxurious apartments called Las Islas de Puerto Marina. Constructed in flamboyant style, they do appear like islands floating on the water.

The marina offers a number of attractions, to suit all age groups, from the new Sea Life Centre and mini-train rides for children, to bars, restaurants and evening entertainment. Another novelty is *Willow*, the Mississippi-style paddleboat; moored here permanently, it is fitted out as a restaurant and nightclub.

Puerto Marina is becoming increasingly popular, especially at weekends, attracting Spaniards and visitors alike. An ultra-modern underwater lighting system has been installed in the waters of the harbour, creating stunning effects.

Up Into the Hills to Mijas

This drive takes you up into the hills through attractive scenery to the picturesque little town of Mijas, passing a couple of other typical Andalucían villages on the return to the coast.

From Benalmádena Costa take the N340 east for a short distance. Turn inland, following the sign to Arroyo de la Miel. In the village turn left at the traffic lights and follow the signs to Tivoli World. Continue up the hill and pass by the Tivoli World Amusement Park on your right to Benalmádena Pueblo. Proceed through the village and follow the signs to Mijas.

A very winding road (with some bad stretches) takes you through lovely pine-clad hillls, with fine views down to the coast. You should reach Mijas some 45 minutes later. Take time to explore this delightful little town, noted for its setting high in the hills.

Take the A387 northwest to Alhaurín el Grande, 17km on.

Drive on through a winding stretch of reddish rocks and pines, with some fine panoramic views on your left and bear right, continuing on the A387, to the village of Alhaurín el Grande. Look for the signs and join the A366 northwest to Coín, which you should reach some 10 minutes later.

After Coín, turn onto the A355, following the signs for Ojén–Marbella, to Monda. Continue on the A355 which now heads south towards Ojén–Marbella.

The road from here to Ojén has a good surface and continuing curves as it passes through an area of rocks and wooded hills. It will take you some 45 minutes to reach Ojén.

Continue south for 8km to the coastal road. Join the N340 and take direction Málaga back to Benalmádena Costa.

Distance
116km

Time
About 5 hours, allowing time to visit Mijas

Start/end point
Banalmádena Costa
⊞ 46C2

Lunch
El Olivar (££)
✉ Avenida Virgen de la Pena, Mijas
☎ 952 48 61 96

Drive up into the hills to the quiet little village of Ojén

49

CASARES (▶ 18, TOP TEN)

COMPETA ✪

Way up in the mountains of La Axarquía, the region east of Málaga, is the small town of Competa, which can be reached by taking the road which leads inland from Torox-Costa.

Competa is noted for its attractive setting, perched atop a mountain ridge surrounded by vineyards. It is one of a number of easily accessible Andalucían towns and villages located in the hills which offer fine views down to the coast. The town is made up of a cluster of whitewashed houses and winding streets. On the main square stands the baroque Iglesia de la Asunción, which features an impressive bell tower.

Competa has quite a sizeable community of foreign residents, a number of whom are involved with craft industries. A big attraction is the lively wine festival which is held each year in August in the main square.

Left and below: *different aspects of the typically Andalucian village of Competa*

* 47E3
* 51km east of Málaga
* Several restaurants (£–££)
* Local services
* Few
* Nerja (▶ 69)
* Noche del Vino (15 Aug)
* Tourist information: Calle La Rampa ☎ 952 55 33 01

Córdoba

Córdoba is one of Andalucía's richest jewels. In addition to the Mezquita or Great Mosque (▶ 22), the city's old quarter of narrow streets with flower-filled balconies and patios allows visitors an insight into the essence of southern Spain. The town lies along the banks of the River Guadalquivir, overlooked by the Sierra de Córdoba. With extremes of heat in the summer and harsh winters, a good time to visit is spring or autumn.

An excellent way of exploring Córdoba is by horse and carriage

Tools found on the banks of the River Guadalquivir suggest that palaeolithic man lived here. Córdoba later became a leading centre of the people of Tartessos and was then conquered by the Carthaginians, the Romans (when it became the capital of Baetica) and the Moors.

In 929, under Moorish rule, the Caliphate of Córdoba was established. With the founding of a university, Córdoba became a renowned

centre of art, culture and learning. This period saw the construction of Córdoba's great Mezquita and other fine examples of Moorish architecture.

Gradually, in the 11th and 12th centuries, Córdoba went into decline. With the breaking up of the Caliphate into small *tarifas* (states), Córdoba came under the jurisdiction of Sevilla. After it fell to the Christians in 1236, the Catholic Monarchs presided here while planning the reconquest of Granada and it was here that Queen Isabella granted Columbus the commission for his voyage of discovery.

The city has many attractions and should be explored on foot. Bear in mind that some of its narrow streets do not easily accommodate pedestrians and cars simultaneously! The Judería (old Jewish Quarter) is a delightful area of tiny streets and white houses. Brilliantly-coloured flowers adorn small squares and patios can be seen through doorways.

➕ 42C3
✉ 187km north of Málaga
🍴 Choice of restaurants (£–£££)
🚌 Estación de Autobuses, Plaza de las Tres Culturas ☎ 957 40 40 40
🚃 Estación de RENFE, Gta Conde Guadalhorce ☎ 957 49 02 02
♿ Few
❓ Easter ceremonies, Flamenco (5–18 May), International Festival of Music, Theatre and Dance (Aug), National Festival of Folklore (Sep)
ℹ Tourist information: Calle Torrijos 10 ☎ 957 47 12 35

What to See in Córdoba

Plaza Campo Santo de los Mártires
957 42 01 51
Tue–Sat 10–2, 6–8; Sun & pub hol 9:30–3. Closed Mon
Few   Cheap (free Tue)

ALCÁZAR DE LOS REYES CRISTIANOS ✪

This Mudéjar-style palace was begun by King Alfonso XI in the early 14th century. Outstanding Roman mosaics, the old Moorish courtyard and baths still remain. This was once the residence of the Catholic Kings, and a one-time Moorish prison.

LA MEZQUITA (► 22, TOP TEN)

Plaza Jerónimo Páez
957 47 40 11
Wed–Sat 9–8, Tue 3–8, Sun & pub hol 9–3. Closed Mon
Few   Cheap

MUSEO ARQUEOLÓGICO PROVINCIAL ✪

Housed in the attractive 16th-century Palacio de los Páez, the museum (957 47 40 11) has a fine collection of objects, ranging from prehistoric to Roman and Moorish times.

Plaza de Potro, 1
957 47 33 45
Wed–Sat 9–8, Tue 3–8, Sun & pub hol 9–3. Closed Mon
Few   Cheap

MUSEO DE BELLAS ARTES ✪

This fine arts museum (957 47 33 45) contains paintings and sculptures by some of Spain's great masters including Goya, Luis Maroles and Alonso.

MUSEO MUNICIPAL TAURINO ✪

The Municipal Bullfighting Museum, which is housed in an elegant 16th-century mansion, has an unusual and fascinating display of items and memorabilia relating to some of Córdoba's most famous bullfighters, including the legendary Manolete.

⊠ Plaza Maimónides 5
☎ 957 20 10 56
🕐 Tue–Sat 10–2 & 6–8, Sun/pub hol 9:30–3. Closed Mon
♿ Few 🎫 Cheap (free Tue)

PALACIO DE VIANA ✪✪

The Viana Palace warrants a visit, if only to see the beautiful patios and gardens of this fine 15th-century building. There are collections of paintings, porcelain, furniture and tapestries worth seeing. Note the spendid Mudéjar ceiling above the stairway to the first floor. Visitors are given a one-hour guided tour.

⊠ Rejas de Don Gome 2
☎ 957 48 01 34
🕐 Mon–Sat 10–1, 4–8; Sun & pub hol 10–2. Closed Wed
♿ Few
🎫 Cheap (free Thu)

TORRE DE LA CALAHORRA ✪

Housed in the 14th-century Moorish fortress across the river, the Museo Histórico (Córdoba City Museum) makes clever use of multi-vision presentations to trace the history of Córdoba at the height of its golden era.

⊠ Puente Romano
☎ 957 29 39 29
🕐 Daily 10–2, 4:30–8:30
♿ None
🎫 Cheap

Left: *Córdoba was once a great cultural centre of Europe*

Below: *the gardens of the Alcázar exude an air of tranquillity*

In the Know

If you only have a short time to visit the Costa del Sol, or would like to get a real flavour of the region, here are some ideas:

Ways To Be A Local

Try to speak some Spanish – even a few basic words and sentences show willing and are usually appreciated.

Shake hands when introduced – it is also normal as a form of greeting or saying goodbye.

Avoid making disparaging remarks or sarcastic jokes – the Spaniards are a proud race.

Try not to be too critical about Spain – leave that to the Spaniards, if they so wish!

Sample local dishes and do not complain if the food is different to back home.

Behave as the locals do with manners and dignity.

Show moderation with drink, like the Spaniards.

Show respect when visiting churches or cathedrals and dress with dignity, particularly in rural areas.

Dress appropriately, according to whether you are on the beach, or sightseeing. Although the customs of covering up have been relaxed, a measure of modesty should be observed.

Avoid Spanish politics, especially if you have a limited knowledge of the subject – it is a touchy area.

Good Places to Have Lunch

Frutos (££)
✉ Frutos Urb Los Alamos, Torremolinos
☎ 952 38 14 50
Try the *jamón Ibérico* for starters and follow up with *cochinillo* (suckling pig).

La Meridiana (£££)
✉ Camino de la Cruz, Marbella
☎ 952 77 61 90
🕐 Wed–Sun. Top reputation for food and service.

Restaurant Plaza (££)
✉ Espada y Urbaneja, Marbella (Casco Antiguo)
☎ 952 86 36 31
Delightful for sitting out. Specialities are *paella* and fish baked in salt.

La Bodega (£)
✉ San Miguel 40, Torremolinos
☎ 952 38 73 37
Local and lively. Excellent seafood, good value.

Mesón El Coto (££)
✉ Ctra San Redro to Ronda, 7km from San Pedro
☎ 952 78 66 88
Attractive setting in the mountains. Charcoal grilled baby lamb, suckling pig and rabbit specialities.

Casa Pedro (££)
✉ Quitapeñas 57, Playa el Palo, Málaga
☎ 952 99 00 13
One of the area's earliest restaurants. Seafood prepared Malaguenian style.

La Langosta (££)
✉ Calle Bulto 53, La Carihuela, Torremolinos
☎ 952 38 43 81
Quality restaurant of long standing, known for seafood and international dishes.

Restaurante Antonio (££)
✉ Calle Muelle Rivera, Puerto Banús
☎ 952 81 35 36
One of the best known restaurants overlooking the port. Speciality is sea bass baked in salt.

El Andaluz (£££)
✉ Hotel Byblos, Urb. Mijas-Golf
☎ 952 47 30 50
Excellent restaurant in attractive surroundings of Byblos Hotel. Special buffet available at lunchtime.

Casa Luque (££)
✉ Plaza Cavana 2, Nerja
☎ 952 52 10 04 Housed in a delightful old Andalucían house. Cuisine from the north of Spain.

Top Activities

Swimming: whether in hotel pools or the sea. Look out for the EU blue flag beaches.
Sailing: all amenities available from the numerous marinas.
Waterskiing: main season Mar–Nov. Facilities available between Málaga and Estepona.
Jetskiing and windsurfing: the season is from Mar–Nov. Equipment and tuition available from hotels. Top spot for windsurfing is Tarifa.
Scuba diving: good area around Nerja; limited on western section of Costa.
Golf: the oft-referred to Costa del Golf has dozens of courses open throughout the year. *The Costa Golf*, published monthly and sold at newsstands, is useful to those interested in playing.

Tennis: many clubs on and around Costa. Most top-class hotels have courts.
Horseriding: many stables up and down the coast and in the hills.
In the Air: Hot air ballooning, flying, gliding, para-gliding and hang-gliding are all popular.
Skiing: the Sierra Nevada ski station is only 100km from the coast. Facilities include good transport, ski lifts, chair lifts and a tourist complex. Season is from Dec to Apr.

Top Street Markets (Baratos)

Selling a variety of goods, ranging from handicrafts and clothes to fruit and vegetables, these are fun to browse around.

Monday: Marbella, by the football stadium
Tuesday: Fuengirola ✉ Recinto Ferial and Nerja, ✉ Antonio Ferrandiz Chanquete
Wednesday: Estepona ✉ Avenida Juan Carlos
Thursday: San Pedro Alcántara ✉ Eduardo Evangelista and Torremolinos ✉ El Calvario
Friday: Benalmádena ✉ Arroyo de Miel
Saturday: Nueva Andalucía ✉ The Bullring and Mijas-Costa, near Euromarket ✉ Urb. El Calypso
Sunday: Estepona ✉ The Port

Top Beaches

Bajondillo, Torremolinos
La Carihuela, Torremolinos
Santa Ana, Benalmádena
La Vibora, between Benalmádena and Fuengirola
Playa de Los Boliches, Los Boliches
Playa de Fuengirola, Fuengirola
La Cala, between Fuengirola and Marbella
Fontanilla, Marbella
La Rada, Estepona
Cala de Maro, east of Nerja

Two locals having a gossip in Estepona

55

✝ 42C1

✉ 82km west of Málaga

🍴 Many restaurants and bars (£–£££)

♿ Few

↔ Puerto Duquesa (13km west) (► 61)

❓ Fiesta de San Isidro (15 May), local festival (early Jul), Fiesta de Virgen del Carmen (16 Jul)

ℹ Tourist information: Avenida de San Lorenzo ☎ 952 80 20 02

Above and right: *its picturesque old town is part of Estepona's charm*

56

ESTEPONA ⭐

Some 36km west of Marbella is Estepona, another of the Costa del Sol's fast developing resorts. It offers the attractions of a long beach, pleasant seafront promenade, a marina and at least three golf courses. It is also a good centre for sailing and windsurfing.

This former fishing village retains a large fleet protected by a harbour which also has moorings for some 400 yachts and pleasure craft. An enjoyable pastime is to wander down to the port early in the morning and watch the fresh catch being sold at the fish market.

The old town dates back to Roman and Moorish times. The focal point is the charming little square of the Plaza de las Flores, entered by four archways of trees. Amid trim orange trees and tropical plants, this is a good place in which to linger over a drink. The surrounding area offers a pleasant stroll through tiny streets lined with picturesque houses. Take a look at the church on Plaza de la Roloj and go down the steps to the Mercado Municipal, a covered market for fruit, vegetables and fresh fish. Above the little town are old castle ruins.

FRIGILIANA ✪

It is well worth taking a short drive of some 6km up into the hills from Nerja to visit Frigiliana. This pretty little village, which has won awards for its looks, spreads its dazzlingly whitewashed houses out over the hills in two sections. The older part is a mass of narrow, cobbled streets winding their way up the hillside with wonderful views over fertile orchards and the coast. Here and there you may come across a donkey patiently carrying its load. Streets and balconies are decked out with colourful flowers. The town has been receiving the growing attention of tourism and an increasing number of shops and restaurants have opened.

One of the last battles between the Christians and the Moors was fought in the area in the 16th century, resulting in victory for the Christians. The tale of this glorious event is related by way of a series of ceramic tiles on the walls of the houses.

FUENTE VAQUEROS ✪

Fuente Vaqueros is home to the **Casa Museo García Lorca**. The museum was the former home of the poet and playwright Federico García Lorca, who was born in Fuente Vaqueros in 1898. Lorca, who spent much time in nearby Granada, became known for the sensitivity of his poetry and the powerful drama of his plays, such as *Yerma*, *Blood Wedding* and *The House of Bernarda Alba*, which continue to be widely produced on stage throughout the world. He was assassinated near Viznar during the Spanish Civil War.

✚ 47E2
✉ 56km east of Málaga
🍴 Some restaurants (££)
🚍 Local
♿ Few
↔ Nerja (➤ 69)
❓ Día de la Cruz (3 May); Feria de San Antonio (13 Jun)
ℹ Tourist information: Calle Puerta del Mar, Nerja
    ☎ 952 52 15 31

Left: *a view of Frigiliana*

Above: *handicrafts for sale in the village*

✚ 47E4
✉ 17km west of Granada

Casa Museo Federico García Lorca

✉ Calle poeta García Lorca
☎ 958 25 84 66
🕐 Tue–Sun summer 10–1 and 4–8 (winter 4–6)
♿ Few 💶 Cheap

59

MA·3·376

✚ 46C2

✉ 29km west of Málaga

🍴 Many restaurants (£–£££)

🚌 Corner Avenida Ramón y Cajal and Calle Alfonso XIII

🚆 RENFE station at Avenida Jesús Santos Rein (half hourly service to Málaga)

♿ Good

↔ Mijas (► 23), Parque Aquático (► 107)

❓ Fiesta de la Virgen del Carmen (16 Jul) in Los Boliches; Romería (late Sep) from Fuengirola; Fería del Rosario (7 Oct)

ℹ Tourist Information: Avenida Jesús Santos Rein 6 ☎ 952 46 76 25

The old art of fishing still plays an important role in the modern lifestyle of today's international resorts

FUENGIROLA ⭐

Some 9km west of Benalmádena Costa is the prominent resort of Fuengirola. It has changed unrecognisably from its earlier days as a peaceful little fishing village. Now the scene is one of solid high-rise apartment blocks and buildings. The old part of the town, however, presents another side of Fuengirola. A lively meeting place is the Plaza de la Constitución, which is dominated by Fuengirola's main church. The old fishermen's district of Santa Fé has plenty of character and high above the town is the old Moorish Castle, Castillo de Sohail.

The Castle, which is thought to have originated with the Romans, was rebuilt by the Moors only to be destroyed in the 15th century during the Christian reconquest of the region. The present structure dates from 1730 when it was again reinforced as protection against the British. The castle is now being converted into a cultural centre. A walk up here is recommended for excellent views of the coast.

Fuengirola is much favoured by northern Europeans who come here for extended stays to escape their native winters. There are many English-run bars and souvenir shops to be found here and in neighbouring Los Boliches. The summer season is always lively; the long sweep of beach especially appeals to families. Fuengirola has several other attractions geared to children, such as the small zoo, an Aquapark at nearby Mijas Costa and the ever-popular Tivoli World up the road.

All kinds of watersports can be enjoyed here too, including sailing, waterskiing and windsurfing. The resort has an attractive yacht club and marina, along with an extended promenade, the Paseo Marítimo, which links Fuengirola, Los Boliches and Carvajal. The former fishing village of Los Boliches has become an extension of Fuengirola, its beach lined with apartment blocks, bars and restaurants. Further east is the small resort of Carvajal, which has so far retained a more Spanish flavour.

Along the Coast to Gibraltar

This drive takes you along the coast through the Sotogrande development to the tiny British colony of Gibraltar.

From Estepona take the N240 coastal road southwest in the direction of Algeciras.

The road follows the coast fairly closely for a while, passing through a string of *urbanizaciones* (developments). Some 10 minutes on you may wish to turn off and take a look at Duquesa Marina (follow the signs), another of the Costa's yacht-filled harbours.

Continue on N340.

You will soon enter the province of Cádiz and the community of Manilva. The road then passes through Sotogrande (known for golf and polo). Shortly after is a turning to Puerto Sotogrande, another marina.

Continue on the N340.

This last section of the coastal road has now been widened into a highway. Ticket offices advertising ferry trips across to Tangier and Centa signal the approach to the ferry ports.

Soon after, turn left onto the N351 and left again following signs to La Linea–Gibraltar, 7km. Drive to La Linea and continue to the border with Gibraltar.

As you can encounter lengthy delays at the border when re-entering Spain, depending on the current political situation, in addition to parking problems in Gibraltar itself, you are strongly advised to leave your car in the parking lot in La Linea. There are ticket machines, with free parking on Sundays. Cross into Gibraltar on foot (you will need to show your passport). Guides are lined up here, ready to take you on a 60–90-minute tour, which includes a drive through town and up to St Michael's Cave where you can see dramatic rock formations. The drive continues steeply up through hairpin bends to see the apes and the sweeping views of the Mediterranean, Atlantic and south to Africa.

Return to La Linea and take the N240 back to Estepona.

The Rock of Gibraltar is an impressive landmark which can be seen for miles along the coast

Distance
105km

Time
About 6 hours, allowing time to visit Gibraltar

Start/end point
Estepona
➕ 42C1

Lunch
Waterfront (££)
✉ Queensway Quay, Gibraltar
☎ 350 45 666

61

🗺 46A2
✉ 120km west of Málaga
🍽 Several restaurants
🚌 Local bus services
♿ Few
↔ Casares (► 18)
❓ Romería San Juan (23 Jun); Fería Virgen de las Nieves (second week Aug); Fiesta de Santo Niño (8, 9 and 10 Sept)
ℹ Tourist information: Avenida de San Lorenzo
☎ 952 80 20 02

GAUCÍN ✪

Situated about 40 minutes away from the coast between Casares and Ronda, Gaucín is yet another of those enchanting little white towns you will come across travelling around the Andalucían countryside. As you approach you will be confronted by a cluster of white-washed houses, topped by red roofs, spread out beneath a cluster of cracked rocks.

The old Moorish fortress, Castillo de Aguila (Eagle's Castle), now partly restored, stands high above the village, forming a silhouette against the backdrop of mountains. From this vantage point there are magnificent views across the valley of the Guadiaro river, reaching out to the coastline as far as the Rock of Gibraltar.

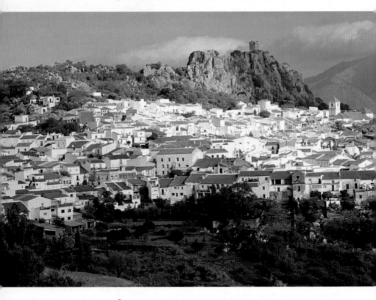

The little white town of Gaucín nestles below a great rock massif crowned by an old Moorish castle

The village is delightful and abounds with colourful flowers and plants. Its narrow streets and one-way system are not conducive to driving, however, and the place is best explored on foot. The daily fish market is always a lively event.

Gaucín makes a good base from which to explore the hinterland, which is dotted about with attractive towns and villages such as Ronda, Grazalema, Casares, Ubrique and Jimena de la Frontera.

Granada

Granada is the capital of its province, the see of an archbishop and a university town. In addition to La Alhambra, with which Granada is so closely associated, the city has much else to commend it: its beautiful setting, built on three hills backed by the snowy peaks of the Sierra Nevada, its historic links with the past and significant religious festivals. A visit to Granada could be made from the coast within a day. However, more time is recommended to explore one of Spain's crowning glories, the last kingdom of the Moors.

Known as Iliberis during the Iberian culture, Granada was taken by the Romans and the Visigoths before its conquest by the Moors in 711. The 11th century saw the decline of the Caliphate of Córdoba and the beginning of the Kingdom of Granada. From the 13th century, until its downfall at the end of the 15th century, Granada flourished as a prosperous cultural centre with the construction of magnificent buildings such as La Alhambra (► 17). In 1492 Granada was taken by the Catholic Monarchs. This marked the end of Moorish rule and Spain's history was changed. Granada continued to prosper during the Renaissance but a decline set in after the repression of a Moorish uprising in the 16th century.

The priority for most visitors is the palace of La Alhambra. Magical as this Moorish palace is, it is surrounded by some equally fascinating places. The summer palace of El Generalife, with its shady avenues, water gardens, fountains and airy gazebos, is a neighbour of La Alhambra that you really should visit. On the slopes of the hill facing La Alhambra is the picturesque old Moorish quarter of Albaicín, a labyrinth of steep, narrow streets and small squares which has changed little with time. To the east rises the hill of Sacramonte, formerly the home of cave-dwelling gypsies.

➕ 47F4
✉ 129km northeast of Málaga
🍴 Variety of bars and restaurants (£–£££)
🚌 Estación de Autobuses, Carretera de Jaén s/n
    ☎ 958 18 50 11
🚉 Estación de FFCC, Avenida de Andaluces
    ☎ 958 27 12 72
♿ Few
❓ Día de la Toma (1, 2 Jan), Semana Santa (Easter), Corpus Christi, International Music and Dance Festival (end Jun, early Jul), Romería (29 Sep), International jazz Festival (Nov)
ℹ Tourist information: Corral del Carbón, Calle del Mariana Pineda 40
    ☎ 958 22 59 90

Close by La Alhambra are the peaceful gardens of the Generalife, former summer palace of Moorish kings

Inside the Capilla Real

✉ Gran Via de Colon
   (Cathedral)
☎ 958 22 92 39
🕐 Mon–Sat 10:30–1, 4–7,
   Sun 11–1, 4–7
🚉 RENFE station Granada
♿ Few
💷 Cheap

✉ Antequerela Alta 11
☎ 958 22 94 21
🕐 Tue–Sat 9:30–3. Closed
   Sun, Mon & pub hols
♿ Few
💷 Cheap

What to See in Granada

CAPILLA REAL ✪✪

The Royal Chapel, sanctioned by the Catholic Monarchs for their burial, was begun in 1506 and completed under the reign of Hapsburg Emperor Charles V in 1521. It has a richly adorned interior. In the chancel, closed by a screen, are the mausoleums of King Ferdinand and Queen Isabella, along with their daughter Juana la Loca and her husband Philip the Fair. A museum reached through the north arm of the transept displays items of historical interest and a fine collection of paintings and sculpture.

CASA MANUEL DE FALLA ✪

Manuel de Falla (1876–1946) was born in Cadiz and taught by Pedrell, the founder of Spain's modern national school of composition. He spent several years in Paris, but drew on his own native musical traditions in works such as the popular ballet music *The Three-Cornered Hat*. The composer lived in this house for a number of years. Items on display relate to his life.

Did you know ?

In January 1492 the Boy King, Boabdil, last Moorish ruler, finally surrendered Granada to the Catholic Monarchs. Looking back on Granada as he went away into exile he is said to have wept, only to be rebuked by his mother with words to the effect that: 'You weep like a woman for what you could not hold as a man.' The spot has ever since been known as the Suspiro del Moro (the Moor's Sigh). It is a few kilometres east of Granada on the road to Motril.

The Boy King Boabdil surrenders the keys of Granada to the Catholics

CATEDRAL ✪
The cathedral was begun in 1528 on the orders of the Catholic Monarchs. Construction was under the great master Diego de Siloé, and continued after his death in 1528. It features a magnificent Capilla Real (Royal Chapel) and has a notable rotunda, with some fine paintings by Alonso Cano, a native of Granada.

✉ Gran Vía de Colon
☎ 958 22 29 59
🕐 Mon–Sat 10:30–1:30, 4–7. Sun/pub hol 4–7. Closed during services
♿ Few
💷 Cheap

MONASTERIO DE LA CARTUJA ✪
This former Carthusian Monastery, which dates back to the 16th century, has a worthwhile collection of paintings and sculpture. Admission is free.

✉ Paseo Cartuja
☎ 958 16 19 32
🕐 Mon–Sat 10–1, 4–8 Sun 10–12, 4–8
💷 Cheap

MUSEO ARQUEOLÓGICO ✪
The museum is housed in the Casa Castril, an elegant Renaissance palace, noted for its delicately carved plateresque doorway. It has a fine collection of ceramics from Roman and Moorish times, in addition to some superb Egyptian vases unearthed in the region.

✉ Carrera del Darro 41
☎ 958 22 56 40
🕐 Wed–Sat 9–8, Tue 3–8, Sun 9–2:30
♿ Few
💷 Cheap

MARBELLA ★★

When mention is made of the Costa del Sol, Marbella comes across as synonymous with the concept of a hedonistic world for the jet set. Since its meteoric rise to fame, Marbella has indeed never ceased to set itself above its fellow resorts along the coast, by continuing to cultivate its image as a playground of the rich and famous with their luxury yachts and glamorous life-styles.

Marbella's development can be traced back to the 1940s, with the founding of the El Rodeo restaurant and inn by the Spanish aristocrat Ricardo Soriano. His nephew, Prince Alfonso Hohenlohe of Liechtenstein, went on to develop a small beach property into the Marbella Club chalet complex for his friends among the international set. This continued to attract celebrities to the area and led to the construction of a string of luxurious hotels which were built along the coast on either side of Marbella town, offering beautiful gardens, pools and sports facilities.

After the halcyon days of the '70s and early '80s, Marbella went into a decline, for a number of reasons, and began to wane in popularity, but it has now received a facelift due largely to the dynamism of its active mayor, Jesús Gil. The remodelling of the Paseo Marítimo, improvements to the beach and a general cleaning-up programme have done much to restore Marbella's image and prestige, with ambitious plans in the offing for future development in the area.

Marbella town has various sides to it, from the thriving commercial centre, with its shops and stores, bars and restaurants, to the coastal promenade, beach, yacht harbour, and the most

---

✚ 46B2

✉ 56km west of Málaga

🍴 Wide range of restaurants, many (£££)

🚌 Bus station, Calle Trapiche ☎ 952 76 44 00

♿ Few

❓ Carnival (pre-Lent), Fería de la Virgen del Carmen (16 Jul), Fería de San Bernabé Patrón (early Jun), Fería de San Pedro (19 Oct)

ℹ Glorieta de la Fontanilla, Paseo Marítimo
☎ 952 77 14 42

Above right: *Marbella continues its expansion to meet demand*

Below: *motorists pass under the arch to Marbella*

attractive section of the Casco Antiguo (Old Town) (► 21). In the centre of Marbella town there are plush apartments overlooking the sea. In spite of the new underground car park beneath the Avenida del Mar, traffic in the town has become increasingly hectic and finding a parking space can present problems.

The remodelled promenade or Paseo Marítimo, which stretches on either side of the town, offers a very pleasant stroll along the seafront. Many improvements have also been made to the long stretch of beach, which is shaded at intervals by clumps of palms and adorned by ornamental elephants. One of Marbella's new acquisitions is the Avenida del Mar. Attractively laid out with flowers and fountains, the avenue links the old Alameda Park to the Paseo Marítimo. The yacht harbour, which has nearly 400 berths, is always an attractive area in which to take a stroll and linger over a drink or a plateful of fresh seafood.

Marbella has several pleasant parks. The oldest, La Alameda, features exotic plants, small trees and fountains. The more recent Constitucíon Park has well kept gardens and an amphitheatre which presents concerts and dances during the summer. In the Arroyo de la Represa Park, also fairly new, is the **Bonsai Museum**, which has a delightful collection of Japanese-style miniature trees.

Bonsai Museum
✉ Arroyo de la Represa Park
🕐 Daily 11:30–2, 5–8:30
💰 Cheap

All kinds of styles make up the face of modern Marbella

The municipality of Marbella covers a 28km stretch of coastline, which stretches from the marina and the residential area of Cabo Pino, east of the town, to Guadalmina out to the west. The section from Marbella to Guadalmina has come to be known as the Golden Mile, so named for the concentration of luxurious hotels, restaurants and golf courses to be found here. Expensive villas with pools, set amidst gardens of lush, tropical vegetation complete the picture.

References to the 'exclusive resort of Marbella' can be misleading as, more often than not, the term applies not to the town, but to the hotels strung out on either side of the town, including the plush Guadalmina development and the Puerto Banús marina. This area is, in effect, the 'playground' of the jet set.

Puerto Banús (➤ 24–5) is officially part of San Pedro de Alcántara (➤ 78, located 3km away) and is usually listed under Nueva Andalucía. However, it is within the community of Marbella and tends to be included in references to the town. It continues to be a place of pure enjoyment and a magnet for yachties. The marina has berths for over 900 and attracts craft of all sizes; millionaires' yachts are a common sight. There are also facilities for many watersports.

Marbella continues to attract the celebrities and stars. The partying goes on but has become less visible as more of the social scene takes place privately. This does not deter many visitors, however, who may well catch sight of some familiar face.

Did you know ?

The most luxurious properties are to be seen in the surroundings of Marbella, particularly in the areas of Nueva Andalucía and Guadalmina. Amidst all this opulence is a palace belonging to King Fahd of Saudi Arabia. Referred to as the White House for its resemblance, in miniature, to its namesake in Washington, it stands out as a landmark in the hills, with a grand mosque, alongside, to keep it company.

MIJAS (➤ 23, TOP TEN)

NERJA ✪✪✪

Nerja lies in a fertile valley of fruit orchards, known mainly for the production of peaches and pomegranates. Its attractive setting amidst cliffs overlooking rocky coves below have earned its reputation as the jewel of the eastern Costa del Sol. Its name is derived from the old Moorish word *naricha*, meaning 'rich in water'. The town started life as a Moorish farming estate during the 10th

✚ 47E2
✉ 52km east of Málaga
🍴 Wide choice of restaurants and bars (£–£££)
🚌 Bus connections
♿ Few
↔ Maro (4km east)

century, a centre of the silk and sugar industries for the area. All reminders of its Moorish past and much of the town were destroyed in the earthquake of 1884.

One of Nerja's best known features is the Balcón de Europa (Balcony of Europe), an attractive tree-lined promenade which extends along a cliff top, offering splendid views of the coast and surrounding mountains. The old

Above and right: Nerja's picturesque coastal setting is its greatest attraction

🎭 Carnival (pre-Lent), Semana Santa (Easter), Cruces de Mayo (3 May), Fiesta de la Virgen del Carmen (16 Jul), Feriá de Nerja (13 Oct)

ℹ️ Tourist information: Puerta del Mar 2 ☎ 952 52 15 31

town rises up the hill behind, in a pleasant cluster of white-washed houses, shops and cafés. There are fine views of the coast and a lively atmosphere. East of the town are the beaches of Calahonda and popular Burriana with further strands stretching away to the west. The Cuevas de Nerja (Nerja caves) are a major tourist draw (► 19). Discovered in 1959, they lie 4km to the east of Nerja.

Although Nerja has grown into an internationally popular resort over the years, it has so far managed to escape the sort of development found along much of its neighbouring western coastline. Most noticeably Nerja has managed to retain its small-town atmosphere. This could well change, however, when Nerja is linked to Málaga by a new motorway. This has been completed as far as Algarrobo, with the latest section to Nerja under construction.

Some 4km east of Nerja lies the little village of Maro. Perched on a clifftop above a small cove, the village offers good views of the coastline. Of interest is the attractive little church of Nuestra Señora de las Maravillas de Maro, and the 4-tiered aqueduct.

Did you know ?

Nerja's famous promenade received its name when King Alfonso XII was touring the area to show sympathy following an earthquake which hit the town on Christmas Day in 1884. While visiting Nerja he stood on the promontory, with its magnificent view of the Mediterranean, and then and there declared it the Balcón de Europa (Balcony of Europe). The name stuck.

Food & Drink

Much of the best natural produce of the Costa del Sol provides the basis for the region's cuisine. Fresh fish, such as sardines, squid, octopus, hake, crayfish and cod are plentiful and widely available. Fruit is produced locally in the fertile orchards to be found to the east of Málaga. Some of the more exotic include peaches, pomegranates, grapes and melons. Olive oil refined in Málaga and olives themselves are of high quality and the cured hams of Trévelez are unequalled.

Local Specialities

As with other tourist destinations, many restaurants on the Costa del Sol provide international cuisine to suit all tastes. But try to search out a menu that includes some typical dishes from the region. You are most likely to find good traditional cooking in smaller eateries inland, away from popular tourist spots.

Fresh grilled fish eaten al fresco

Popular starters are two chilled soups: the tomato-based *gaspacho Andaluz* and *ajo blanco* which is made from garlic and almonds and served with grapes. *Potajes* are thick soups, often based on potatoes and vegetables, suited to mountain weather. *Sopa de rape* is among the many excellent fish soups you can find.

Typical of coastal cooking is *fritura malagueña*, an assortment of fried fish. Other dishes to look out for are cod *à la Málaga*, fish chowders, casserole of dogfish, cockles, crayfish and prawns grilled or served *al pil-pil* (sizzling with garlic). Roasted sardines and fresh anchovies can also be delicious and rice dishes such as a *risotto à la*

Did you know ?

Chiringuitos *is the name given to beach bars and restaurants. They are to be found all along the coast, ranging from simple open air huts, where the emphasis is casual, to more sophisticated eateries. These are often very good places to sample good traditional Spanish dishes, with an emphasis on fresh fish and seafood, either fried or grilled and served with a simple salad.*

marinera (seafood) or *paella* are usually a good bet.

Habas à la rondeña (broad beans Ronda-style), *pimientos à la malaguena* (peppers Málaga-style) are other local dishes to sample. *Puchero* is a sort of country casserole with chickpeas.

Up in the hills above Málaga you can come across tasty varieties of sausages from the different regions. Try the *morcillas* of Antequera, *embutidos* from Ronda and *chorizo* produced in Benaofán. *Conejo* (rabbit) or *pollo al ajillo* (chicken with garlic) are popular dishes and kid is also a delicacy here. The Alpujarras is famous for its hams and produces succulent pork dishes, such as suckling pig.

Above: *take-away stalls for fruit and drinks are plentiful*

Below: *Mijas has its share of food stalls*

Worth a mention among the desserts are *yemas del tajo*, based on egg yolks and sugar, *dulce de membrillo*, made from quinces and there is always the ubiquitous *flan* (crême caramel). A very typical way to round off a meal, however, is with the fresh fruit of the season.

Wine

Málaga is known for its wines. Although there are dry varieties it is famous primarily for its sweet wines, produced from the grapes of Antequera, La Axarquía.

Some excellent sweet dessert wines are also grown in the vineyards around Competa where it is possible to try wine-tasting. Further inland, some very acceptable wines are produced in the Montilla-Moriles area within the province of Córdoba. Although not a local product, a jug of *sangría* (red wine, fruit and lemonade), served chilled with ice, is a pleasant accompaniment to a meal on a warm day. A popular liqueur is *aguardiente de Ojén*.

✚ 47D2
✉ 12km east of Málaga
❓ Fiesta de la Virgen del la Candelaria (1–3 Feb), Fiesta de la Virgen del Carmen (16 Jul), Fiesta de Verano (22–25 Aug)
ℹ Pasaje de Chinitas 4, Málaga ☎ 952 21 34 45

✚ 46A2
✉ 118km northwest of Málaga
🍴 Many restuarants (£–£££)
🚌 Buses from Algeciras, Málaga (via Bobadilla)
♿ Few
❓ Pedro Romero Festival (► 116)
ℹ Plaza de España 1 ☎ 952 87 12 72

Above: shrine of the Virgen del Carmen in Rincón de la Victoria

Right: Ronda's bullring is one of the oldest in Spain

RINCÓN DE LA VICTORIA ✪

Lying some 12km east of Málaga, Rincón de la Victoria is a fast developing resort. It offers a pleasant new seafront promenade, some modest accommodation, an 18-hole golf course, riding, tennis and boats for hire. The resort has a reputation for good fish restaurants, a speciality being a small sardine-type fish known as *victorianos* and *coquinas* (clams). The Wednesday market is always a great event.

RONDA ✪✪✪
(Puente Nuevo ► 26 and Town Walk ► 76)

Of major interest is the imposing collegiate church, Iglesia de Santa Maria Mayor. Formerly a 13th-century mosque, it was rebuilt as a church by Ferdinand the Catholic and shows a mixture of styles. Near by is the 14th-century minaret of San Sebastian. A short walk will take you to the Palacio de Mondragón. Built in 1314 by the Moorish king of Ronda, it long served as a residence for kings and governors.

Other monuments include the Casa del Gigante (Giant's House), a 14th-century Moorish palace, the attractive 18th-century Palacio del Marqués de Salvatierra (Palace of the Marquis Salvatierra) and la Casa del Rey Moro (House of the Moorish King). There are splendid views from its gardens, with nearby steps leading down to the river. Further down are two old bridges known as the Puente Viejo (Old Bridge) and Puente Arabe (Arab Bridge).

Ronda has long-standing associations with bullfighting. The bullring, which is located near the Puente Nuevo, was built in 1785 and is the oldest in Spain. It was here that the rules of modern bullfighting were laid down by Francisco Romero, whose grandson Pedro Romero went on to become one of Spain's most famous matadors. The bullring, now owned by Antonio Ordoñez, another of the greats, is used only for special fiestas. The bullfighting museum behind the ring contains glittering costumes, gear and a wealth of photographs relating to the world of bullfighting.

Ronda is a city with a romantic past and it has long been a source of inspiration to artists and personalities. Ernest Hemingway spent much time down here and formed a close friendship with Ordoñez. Ronda is believed to have been used in part as a setting for two of his books *For Whom the Bell Tolls* and *Death in the Afternoon*. Another visitor and friend of Ordoñez was actor Orson Welles, whose ashes are scattered over the nearby ranch of the famous bullfighter.

Some 20km southwest of Ronda is the **Cueva de la Pileta** (Pileta Cave), which has significant prehistoric rock paintings of animals, outlined in black and red, believed to date back to over 25,000 years ago. The illustrated figures include bison, deer, horses and a large fish.

Cueva de la Pileta
✚ 46A2
✉ 20km southwest of Ronda
🕐 Open daily 10–1 and 4–6; visits with guide last about one hour
♿ Few ✋ Cheap

Did you know ?

The Austrian romantic poet Rainer María Rilke, who came here in 1913 to recuperate from an illness, wrote of Ronda: 'Everywhere I sought the dream of city and at last I have found it.' His room at the Reina Victoria Hotel has been kept much as it was and preserved as a tiny museum. A key may be requested at reception to visit the room, which contains some photographs and verses written by Rilke during his stay. His sensitivity is well portrayed in the statue which stands in the garden.

A Walk in & Around Ronda

Distance
4km

Time
2–3 hours

Start/end point
Plaza de España
✚ 46A2

Lunch
Pedro Romero (££)
✉ Virgen de la Paz 18
☎ 952 87 11 10

This walk starts in the Plaza de España and takes you across the bridge to explore the old town of Ronda.

From the Plaza de España walk towards the Puente Nuevo (New Bridge).

Take a walk around the Parador, on your right, for spectacular views of the gorge.

Return and cross over the bridge into the old sector.

Take a good look down into the ravine as you pass. A right turn down Calle Tenorio will take you into a network of narrow streets and neat white houses to the Plaza del Campillo, which offers sweeping views.

Keep walking and at the far end look for steps leading down the hill.

A short walk down will reveal the spectacle of Ronda's houses perched on the clifftop. A further walk down will provide you with the classic view of the bridge, but it's a long climb up!

Back up again take the small street ahead to the Plaza Mondragón.

On the right is the Palacio de Mondragón, once a Moorish palace. A left turn leads to a square which is dominated by the impressive Colegiata de Santa María la Mayor. Near by is the minaret of San Sebastian.

Exit into Calle Armiñán and turn left back towards the Puente Nuevo. Cross the road, turn right along Ruedo D. Elvira.

Below the town are plenty of walking areas from which to appreciate Ronda's spectacular setting above

Take a look at the Palacio del Marqués de Salvatierra. A short walk up Calle Santo Domingo leads past the old palace known as the Casa del Rey Moro, where the gardens offer a spectacular view of the gorge.

Rejoin Calle Armiñán and cross back over the bridge to the Plaza de España.

The small white town of Salobreña reaches up the hillside to the old Moorish castle known as El Capricho.

SALOBREÑA ⊗

Some 13km east of Almuñecar is the attractive little town of Salobreña, now within the stretch of coast known as the Costa Tropical. It lies a short distance from the coast among fruit orchards and sugarcane plantations.

Salobreña features a cluster of whitewashed houses sprawling up the hill, dominated by the old Moorish *alcázar* known as El Capricho. The castle has been well restored and offers magnificent views of the coast, surrounding countryside and the beautiful peaks of the Sierra Nevada. Also worth a visit is the 16th-century church of Nuestra Señora del Rosario, which was built on the site of an old mosque.

Much of Salobreña's charm lies in the fact that it remains relatively unspoilt, with few hotels and restaurants. It provides a good gateway to Granada, however, and can receive quite an influx of visitors, especially at weekends. From here it is only 4km further along the coast to Motril, principally known as a commercial centre for sugarcane and chemicals. Take a look at the Sanctuary of Our Lady of the Head, which stands atop the hill. Enthusiasts enjoy the golf course, located between the two.

47F2
93 km east of Málaga
Choice of restaurants (£–£££)
Bus connections
Few
Almuñecar (13km west, ➤ 42)
Semana Santa (Easter), Fiesta de San Juan y San Pedro (end Jul), Fiesta de Nuestra Señora del Rosario (early Oct)
Tourist information: Plaza de Goya s/n ☎ 958 61 03 14

77

A quiet spot in the heart of San Pedro de Alcántara, a town which has been nicely rejuvenated

🗓 46B1
✉ 70km west of Málaga
🍴 Choice of restaurants and bars (£–£££)
♿ Few
ℹ Tourist information: Calle Marques del Duero, 69
☎ 952 78 52 52

SAN PEDRO DE ALCÁNTARA ✪

San Pedro Alcántara has undergone a facelift in recent years, with pleasing results. A development programme incorporating a new coastal promenade and beach improvements, stretching from Puerto Banús to Guadalmina, has given it a boost as an increasingly popular resort.

On the northern side of the coastal road is the small town itself, which has a neat, pleasant appearance. The Calle Marqués del Duero, attractively shaded by orange trees and palms, and lined with shops and cafés, leads up the hill to the small square of Plaza de la Iglesia adorned by a fountain. Adjacent to the town hall is San Pedro's parish church. Its white façade framed by two palm trees makes an attractive picture.

San Pedro is the first centre in Spain to have introduced the sport of cable skiing, which involves the water skier being towed by cable for long distances.

Three archaeological sites in the vicinity are worth exploring: the 6th-century Visigoth Basílica de Vega del Mar, the Villa Romana de Río Verde, remnants of a Roman villa from the 1st century, and Las Bovedas where the remains of old Roman thermal baths can be seen.

🗓 42C1
✉ 100km west of Málaga
🍴 Wide choice
🚌 Bus connections
♿ Few
❓ San Roque Annual Fair (early Sep), Sotogrande golf tournaments, polo matches (Jul, Aug, Sep)
ℹ Avda 20 Abril s/n, La Línea ☎ 956 76 99 50

SAN ROQUE/SOTOGRANDE ✪

This is *the* place for big time golfers and is said to feature Spain's highest proportion of registered golfers in any one centre. Among the four golf courses, the Valderrama Robert Trent Jones Course played host to the 1997 Ryder Cup. Polo is also played here during the summer and the Sotogrande Marina is another attraction.

The little town is an attractive centre in itself with narrow streets and plenty of flowers and plants. The lively cafés and restaurants of the Campamento area appeal to a younger crowd.

A Tour of Andalucían Towns & Villages

This drive takes you into the rugged landscape of the Serranía de Ronda and through several of the region's most attractive mountain towns.

From the east side of San Pedro de Alcántara, take the turning to Ronda (▶ 74).

The C339/A473, (Ruta de la Serranía de Ronda) is fairly wide and has a good surface as it twists its way up into the mountains offering fine views. The route takes you through pine forests, rocks and white cliffs, until Ronda comes into view, about an hour later (50km). Allow time to visit Ronda and have some lunch at the restaurant which offers a dramatic view of the steep cliff on which the town is built.

Return through the old town and take the C341, in the direction of Algeciras, to Gaucín(▶ 62).

This section passes through barren hills and rocks and wide open vistas and includes a bad stretch of road. Take a look at the delightful white hillside town of Gaucín.

Join the MA539, direction Manilva–Algeciras. Some 16km on take a sharp left turn to the photogenic town of Casares (▶ 18).

This road leads shortly to a stunning view of this white Andalucían town sprawled over the hillside. Continue towards the town and take a left fork uphill for an even more spectacular sight of the town, crowned by the old fortress.

Follow the signs to Estepona and take the old road, which winds its way down through fertile country to the coast. You should reach Estepona some 25 minutes later (▶ 56). Rejoin N340 and head east back to San Pedro.

Distance
145km

Time
About 8 hours

Start/end point
San Pedro de Alcántara
✚ 46B1

Lunch
Hotel-Restaurante Don Miguel (££)
✉ Villanueva 4 y 8, Ronda
☎ 952 87 10 90

As a contrast to the golfing world of neighbouring Sotogrande, San Roque has a few attractions of its own

79

Sevilla

Sevilla is the capital of Andalucía and Spain's fourth largest city. The city is dominated by La Giralda and the great cathedral that this minaret tower adjoins (➤ 20). Various cultures have left their mark here, from the Romans to the Moors and the Christians. According to legend, Sevilla was founded by Hercules. Its history has been captured by an early carving on the Jerez Gate: 'Hercules built me, Caesar surrounded me with walls and towers, the King Saint took me.'

The town of Hispalis, which may have been Iberian and Phoenician, was taken over by the Romans around 205BC. Under Julius Caesar the town flourished. The judicial district of Colonia Julia Romula was established, the city was walled and it became the capital of Roman Baetica. Two Roman emperors, Hadrian and Trajan, were born in nearby Italica where Roman ruins can be seen. Some fine Roman artefacts found here are on display in Sevilla's archaeological museum.

In the 5th century it became the capital of the Visigoths. In 712 the town was captured by the Moors and called Izvilla, from which its present name is derived. Many fine buildings were erected during this period of Moorish rule.

In 1248 it was conquered by Ferdinand III of Castile. In the 13th century Pedro I (known as the Cruel) had the Alcázar built. But it was the discovery of America which brought fame and prosperity to Sevilla, when Christopher Columbus returned here from his first voyage in 1493. In the 16th and 17th centuries the port became the most important in Spain. During this period, often described as Spain's Golden Age, the Sevilla school of painters brought great prestige to the city.

Sevilla is a city to explore on foot with the cathedral a good focal point from which to start. You will discover elegant mansions, attractive squares and lovely parks, such as the Maria Luisa Park and Murillo gardens. Over the bridge is the Triana area, home of the gypsy population.

Well known as the setting for *Carmen* and other famous operas, Sevilla has long had a romantic image. In the spring, when the heady scent of orange blossom gives Sevilla a special atmosphere, the unique celebrations of Semana Santa (Holy Week) and the exuberant Fería de Sevilla take place (➤ 115).

The recent upturn in Spain's fortunes was exemplified here in 1992 when Sevilla hosted the World Fair.

42B2

219km northwest of Málaga

Huge choice of restaurants and *tapas* bars for which the city is famed

Bus stations: Prado de San Sebastián ☎ 954 41 71 11 & Plaza de Armas ☎ 954 90 80 40

Few

Estación de FFCC Santa Justa, Avenida Kansas City s/n ☎ 954 54 02 02

Semana Santa (Easter), Fería de Sevilla (2 weeks after Easter), Corpus Christi, Fiesta de la Virgen de los Reyes (15 Aug)

Avenida de la Constitucion 21 B ☎ 954 22 14 04

Left: *horse and carriage in the Maria Luisa Park, Sevilla*

Barrio Santa Cruz
The medieval quarter of the Barrio Santa Cruz is a delightful maze of narrow streets and houses adorned with wrought iron balconies, decked with flowers. Spring is an especially good time in which to enjoy the open air cafés and restaurants.

River Walk
A pleasant walk along the banks of the River Guadalquivir evokes a strong sense of Sevilla's past and takes you past the baroque church of La Magdalena, the Fine Arts Museum and La Maestranza, one of Spain's outstanding bullrings. The Torre del Oro (Golden Tower), built by the Moors, is now a small museum.

81

What to See in Sevilla

CASA DE PILATOS ✪✪✪
This grand palace, started in the late 15th century, now contains a fine collection of paintings, sculpture and Mudéjar tiles on two floors and in a large patio built in the Moorish style. Other rooms give an insight into the way of life of the family who lived here.

MUSEO ARQUEOLÓGICO ✪✪✪
Housed in the Renaissance palace built for the 1929 Ibero-America Exhibition, the Museo Arqueológico (Archeological Museum) has a fine collection of objects from prehistory and the Moorish culture. Outstanding among its exhibits is the Carombolo Treasure; dating from the 7th century this includes gold jewellery from the Tartessos civilisation.

Plaza Pilatos 1
954 22 52 98
Daily 9–7
Good
Moderate

Plaza de América
954 23 24 01
Wed–Sat 9–8, Tue 3–8
Sun & pub hols 9–2:30
Closed Mon
Few
Cheap

MUSEO DE BELLAS ARTES (FINE ARTS MUSEUM) ✪✪✪

Housed in the former Convento de la Merced, the museum contains a splendid collection of fine art with paintings and sculpture, ceramics and weapons. Room V contains works of art by some of the great Spanish masters, including Zurbarán and Murillo.

⊠ Plaza Museo 9
☎ 954 22 07 90
🕐 Wed–Sat 9–8, Tue 3–8, Sun & pub hols 9–3. Closed Mon
♿ Few
💰 Cheap

REALES ALCÁZARES ✪✪✪

Formerly a fortress built by the Moors, this was enlarged in the 11th century by the Almohades, with the Patio del Yeso and Patio del Crucero. Later a series of palaces was built over and around the ruins by the Christian kings, from Fernando III to Pedro the Cruel, who ordered the building of the Mudéjar Palace, star of the complex.

⊠ Plaza del Triunfo
☎ 954 22 71 63
🕐 Tue–Sat 9:30–7, Sun 9:30–5. Closed Mon
♿ Few
💰 Moderate

Far left: *magnificent Mudéjar carvings are an attractive feature of the Reales Alcázares in Sevilla*

Left: *the restaurants and bars around the cathedral are always lively on a warm Sevillian evening*

83

Moorish-looking Tarifa is the continent's southern-most town

🕇 42B1
✉ 21km west of Algeciras
🍴 Choice of restaurants (£–£££)
🚌 Bus connections with Algeciras
♿ Few
↔ Roman ruins at Baelo Claudia at Bolonia (14km northwest on N340, 9km off main road to Bolonia Cove)
❓ Día de los Reyes (6 Jan), Carnival (pre-Lent), Romería del Consejo (15 May), Fiesta de San Juan (24 Jun), Fiesta de la Virgen del Carmen (16 Jul), National Folk Music Festival (early Aug), Fiesta de Nuestra Señora de la Luz (early Sep)
ℹ Paseo de la Alameda
☎ 956 68 09 93

TARIFA ⭐

To stand on the Punta de Tarifa is to be at the south-ernmost point of Europe, with the coast of the African continent only 14km away. Located on the fringe of the Costa del Sol, Tarifa has a totally different flavour about it which in itself makes a visit worthwhile.

The town has played an important role in the history of the Iberian peninsula. It was named after Tarif Ibn Malik, the Moorish leader who in 710 arrived here from north Africa with a small band of men and took possession of the area. This led to the larger invasion which took place the following year and the subsequent Moorish conquest of most of present-day Spain. Tarifa was taken by the Christians in 1292 but the siege was maintained for the next couple of years.

Entrance to the town, which is encircled by walls, is through a Moorish gate. With its dazzling white houses and maze of narrow, winding streets, Tarifa retains a distinctive Moorish look. The port offers a good view of the old Moorish castle above the town, which is in the hands of the Spanish Navy and not open to the public.

Tarifa is blessed by a long expanse of sandy beach backed by pine trees. This marks the meeting point of the Mediterranean and the Atlantic and the strong winds which sweep across the sand create excellent conditions for windsurfing in the bay. The place has now become a top centre for the sport, with competitions attracting an international crowd.

TORRE DEL MAR ✪

Located in the eastern part of the Costa de Sol, Torre del Mar is the beach resort of Vélez-Málaga, capital of the Axarquía region.

There are unsubstantiated claims that Torre del Mar once formed part of an ancient Greek settlement known as Mainake which is believed to have been destroyed by the Carthaginians, prior to the arrival of the Romans. These days the town consists primarily of a long beach lined with a string of high-rise apartment blocks catering mainly for summer visitors.

One of the resort's most pleasant features is the extended esplanade which follows the coast, to reach the Marina of Caleta de Vélez. With over 200 berths, it presents an attractive scene of boats and yachts, offering sailing and a variety of other watersports. Its lively cafés and restaurants also provide a good place in which to idle the time away. Another bonus is the good seafood served here in numerous eateries.

- ✚ 47D2
- ✉ 30km east of Málaga
- 🍴 Choice of restaurants and bars (£–£££)
- 🚌 Bus connections
- ♿ Few
- ↔ Vélez-Málaga (5km inland, ▶ 90)
- ❓ Fiestas at Vélez-Málaga
- ℹ Tourist information: Avenida de Andalucía 119 ☎ 952 54 11 04

Above: *some boats at Torre del Mar bear colourful decorations*

Left: *the regular mending of his nets is essential to the livelihood of every local fisherman*

✚ 46C2

✉ 12km west of Málaga

🍴 Many pubs, restaurants, bars (£–£££)

🚆 Half-hourly to Málaga (25 minutes) and Fuengirola

♿ Few

↔ Málaga (➤ 28), Puerto Deportivo at Benalmádena (➤ 46)

❓ Carnival (pre-Lent), Feria de Verdiales (Mar), Easter, Fiesta de la Virgen del Carmen (16 Jul), Romería San Miguel Patron (29 Sep), Día del Turista (early Sep)

ℹ Plaza de las Comunidades Autónomas, s/n (Playa de Bajondillo) ☎ 952 37 19 09

TORREMOLINOS ✪

Torremolinos, lying only 8km west of Málaga airport, heralds the start of the most developed part of the coast. To many, this stretch of coast, lined with high-rise apartment blocks and development as far as Estepona, represents the real Costa del Sol.

Until some 50 years ago Torremolinos was a tiny fishing village named for its flour mills (*torre molinos*), a few of which can still be seen today. It began to grow as a holiday resort in the 1950s, when the building of luxury hotels got under way, and it became one of the first places on this coast to cater for mass tourism. Its proximity to Málaga airport is a point in its favour. At the height of summer the resort has a great appeal for the younger set, with a reputation for its hectic night life. Out of season, however, it takes on a different character. Now practically a suburb of Málaga, the atmosphere is much more Spanish, especially at weekends, with an air of friendliness and welcome.

Surrounded by numerous bars and restaurants, Calle San Miguel is the main artery of the town. This smartly paved pedestrianised street is lined with boutiques and shops with a great variety of goods on offer, attracting a constant flow of people. The Cuesta del Tajo, at the end of San Miguel, leads down a steep flight of steps through the old fishing district of El Bajondillo. This is a popular, picturesque area lined with restaurants and market-style kiosks, selling tourist goods. Down at the bottom is the beach of El Bajondillo.

The beach area shows another side of Torremolinos. With massive hotels, apartment blocks, bars and restaurants, this area is packed during the summer. To the left, the Playa de Bajondillo gives way to the beaches of Playmar and Los Almos. To the right, beyond the Castillo de Santa Clara, lie the beach areas of La Carihuela and Montemar.

Did you know ?

A pioneer of the development of Torremolinos was an Englishman. George Langworthy (Don Jorge or El Señorito Inglés as he was called by the local people) made history when in 1930 he opened up his home, the Hacienda Santa Clara, as a residence for foreigners, creating a centre for the needy. He grew to be held in great esteem by the local people and, after his death, a street was named for him and a monument erected in his honour.

The seafront promenade, Paseo Marítimo, extends east to Playamar and west to La Carihuela, now continuing as far as Benalmádena Costa. The walk to La Carihuela offers pleasant sea views and some dramatic rock formations, before entering the old fishing village of La Carihuela, which is a delightful area of pictureque little houses and streets. It has a good reputation for excellent fish and seafood restaurants. In summer, the *chiringuitos* (beach bars) are well worth sampling.

The area of El Calvario is less known to the average tourist. Located to the north of the main road which cuts through Torremolinos, it offers a quieter area of small streets and bars, with an appeal to those who prefer to be away from the bustle of the centre. Located in the Calle Maria Barrabino is *The Galloping Major* (splendidly translated as *El Comandante Galopando*). Opened in 1964, it is famous for being the Costa del Sol's first pub.

Top: *Torremolinos is one of the coast's liveliest resorts*

Above: *La Carihuela Beach is famed for its beach bars*

87

A Drive to Antequera

Distance
125 km

Time
About 6 hours

Start/end point
Torremolinos
✚ 46C2

Lunch
Chaplin (££)
✉ Calle San Agustín 3,
Antequera
☎ 952 84 30 34

This drive offers some striking scenery, taking you first to Antequera and continuing to the bizarre boulders in the El Torcal National Park.

From Torremolinos turn onto the N340 towards Málaga. Passing the airport on your left, continue on the Málaga ring road (Ronda de Málaga). Turn right to Antequera and follow the signs.

After the turn off to Finca de la Concepción this excellent highway climbs up through the hills of the Montes de Málaga, scattered with olive groves and tiny white houses. As you approach Antequera strange rock shapes rise from the fertile plains, noticeably the striking form of the so-called Peña de los Enamorados (Lovers' Rock). About an hour after departure you should enter Antequera (➤ 44). Allow time to explore this attractive city of churches and convents.

The expansion of Torremolinos from tiny fishing village to popular resort can be observed from the hills of Mijas

Take the Calle de la Legión, in a southerly direction and a few moments out of town, pause to admire the magnificent views of Antequera on your left, backed by the distinctive form of the Peña de los Enamorados. Take the C3310, following the signs to Torcal.

The road winds through a barren landscape of rocks and boulders for about half an hour before reaching a right turn to Parque Natural del Torcal de Antequera. As you drive through the park, the rocks and boulders become increasingly curious, until the whole landscape appears positively lunar-like. The road ends some 15 minutes later by a small hut; walking trails start from here.

Rejoin the C3310 and continue south to the coast and return to Torremolinos.

TORROX COSTA ⭐

Along the eastern end of the Costa del Sol, situated between Torre del Mar and Nerja, is the resort of Torrox Costa. Torrox consists basically of a long stretch of beach, backed with modern apartment blocks, sympathetically designed with reflections of the Moorish style of architecture.

The resort has been developed primarily for summer visitors, when it bustles. The beach offers a number of watersports, while an extended promenade offers the visitor a pleasant stroll along the seafront, with a reasonable choice of restaurants, bars and shops.

You might like to take a look at the church of La Encarnación and the Hermitage of Nuestra Señora de las Nieves, both of which still retain traces of Moorish influences. Scattered along the coast are a few old watchtowers and small fortresses, going back to the times when there was a threat of pirate invasion.

Some 4km inland lies the old town of Torrox; built up the steep slopes of the hill, its whitewashed houses make an attractive pattern.

- **✚** 47E2
- **✉** 47km east of Málaga
- **🍴** Choice of restaurants and bars (£–£££)
- **🚌** Bus connections
- **♿** Few
- **↔** Competa (18km north) (► 50), Nerja (6km east) (► 69)
- **❓** Carnival (pre-Lent), La Cruz de Mayo (2 May), Fiesta de San Juan (23–24 Jun), Fiesta de la Virgen de la Nieves (5 Aug), local fair (4–7 Oct)
- **ℹ** Centro Internacional, bloque 79 ☎ 952 53 02 25

Torrox, above, and the beach at Torrox Costa, right

47D2
34km east of Málaga
Many restaurants (£–£££)
Bus connections
Few
Nerja (➤ 69)
Ayuntamiento ☎ 952 50 01 00

VÉLEZ-MÁLAGA ⊗

The small town of Vélez-Málaga lies 5km inland from Torre del Mar, surrounded by subtropical vegetation. Capital of La Axarquía, it is the centre of an agricultural region known for its production of strawberries and vineyards, which produce the muscatel grapes from which the famous Málaga wines are made. It is also a centre for the processing of olive oil and sugarcane. Ceramics feature among other industries. If you are here on a Thursday, take time to wander around its weekly market, always an enjoyable experience.

The town is crowned by a 13th-century Moorish castle which has been well restored. There are good views of the surrounding countryside from up here. The oldest part of the town, known as Arrabal de San Sebastián, is a picturesque area of narrow streets. You will also come across attractive mansions built during the 16th and 17th centuries. Of special note, among the several churches to be found in the town, is the 15th-century church of Santa María la Mayor, which shows the Mudéjar style. This was the first building to be erected by the Christians, following their victory over the Moors here in 1487.

Above: *some attractive façades can be seen in Vélez-Málaga*

Right: *a rooftop view of the town from its well-restored Moorish castle*

Where To...

Eat and Drink   92–7
Stay   98–101
Shop   102–5
Take the Children   106–7
Be Entertained   108–16

Restaurants in Costa del Sol & Beyond

Prices

Prices are approximate, based on a three-course meal for one without drinks or service:

£ = up to 1,650 ptas
££ = 1,650–4,400 ptas
£££ = over 4,400 ptas

Eating Costs

The cost of eating out along the coast is wide open. In the more fashionable restaurants prices can be on a par with top international restaurants anywhere. However, with careful selection, you can eat very well in and around the coast at reasonable cost, with a variety of restaurants offering fare from other countries.

Antequera

El Carmen (£)

Traditional bar/restaurant with a wide choice of *tapas*.

✉ Plaza del Carmen 3 ☎ 952 70 07 90 🕐 Lunch and dinner

Las Pedrizas (££)

Known for its traditional Andalucían cooking.

✉ Carretera Málaga–Madrid at km 527 ☎ 952 75 12 50 🕐 Lunch and dinner

Arroyo de la Miel

Mesón del Virrey (£££)

In a pleasant old building. Known for good traditional cooking with emphasis on meat dishes. Summer terrace. Popular at weekends.

✉ Avenida de la Constitución 87 ☎ 952 44 35 99 🕐 Lunch and dinner, closed Wed

Ventorillo de la Perra (£££)

Housed in an 18th-century inn. Cosy, attractive patio with plants. Spanish and international dishes.

✉ Avenida Constitución ☎ 952 44 19 66 🕐 Lunch and dinner, closed Mon

Benalmádena Costa

Alonso (££)

Known for its good service and consistent menu.

✉ Carretera Nacional 340 ☎ 952 44 34 35 🕐 Lunch and dinner

Malagueto Puerto (££)

Offers good grilled meats and a wide selection of fish dishes. Bream, baked in salt, can be a good bet.

✉ Puerto marina ☎ 952 44 00 04 🕐 Lunch and dinner

El Verdadero (££)

Friendly atmosphere, good seafood dishes and quality service.

✉ Puerto Marina ☎ 952 56 43 27 🕐 Lunch and dinner

Benalmádena Pueblo

Casa Fidel (££)

Rustic atmosphere with large fireplace. International cuisine.

✉ Maestra Ayala 1 ☎ 952 44 82 21 🕐 Lunch and dinner, closed Tue

La Rueda (££)

Good value international menu. Specialises in chicken and lamb.

✉ Calle San Miguel 2 ☎ 952 44 82 21 🕐 Lunch and dinner, closed Tue

Córdoba

El Caballo Rojo (£££)

Among the top restaurants of Córdoba. By the mosque with attractive Andalucían décor. Some traditional dishes.

✉ Cardenal Herrero 28 ☎ 957 47 53 75 🕐 Lunch and dinner

El Churrasco (££)

Long-standing restaurant and lively *tapas* bar. Centrally located with attractive patio. Known for grilled meats.

✉ Romero 16 ☎ 957 29 08 17 🕐 Lunch and dinner, closed Aug

Estepona

La Casa de mi Abuela (£££)

Specialises in Argentinian grilled meat.

✉ Calle Caridad 54 ☎ 952 79 19 67 🕐 Lunch and dinner, closed Mon

La Fuente (£££)

Cosy atmosphere and attractive patio. Mainly international cuisine.

✉ Calle San Antonio 48
☎ 952 79 29 79 🕒 Lunch and dinner, closed Tue

Costa del Sol (££)
Good value French cuisine in informal friendly atmosphere. Look out for the dish of the day.
✉ Calle San Roque, 23 ☎ 952 80 11 01 🕒 Lunch and dinner, closed Mon lunch, Sun dinner

La Cacerola (££)
Popular restaurant with some good basic international dishes and good value menus.
✉ Pasaje Victoria ☎ 952 79 38 83 🕒 Dinner only, closed Thu

Frigiliana
The Garden Bar (££)
A popular restaurant with locals offering a casual atmosphere and attractive views.
✉ In the old part of the town. Look for the signs. ☎ 952 53 31 85 🕒 Lunch and dinner

Fuengirola
La Cazuela (££)
Small restaurant housed in former fisherman's cottage. Look out for good value dish of the day.
✉ Miguel Marqués 8 ☎ 952 47 46 34 🕒 Lunch and dinner

La Langosta (£££)
Restaurant of long standing, known for seafood and international dishes.
✉ Calle Francisco Cano s/n ☎ 952 47 50 49 🕒 Lunch and dinner, closed Mon

Portofino (££)
Italian specialities and international dishes in this restaurant on the seafront.
✉ Edificio Perla, Paseo Marítimo 29 ☎ 952 47 06 43 🕒 Lunch and dinner, closed Mon

Valparaiso (£££)
International cuisine for that special night out with dancing.
✉ Carretera de Mijas ☎ 952 48 59 75 🕒 Lunch and dinner, closed Sun

Granada
Alacena de las Monjas (££)
Centrally situated and specialising in local cuisine.
✉ Plaza Padre Suárez ☎ 958 22 40 28 🕒 Lunch and dinner, closed Sun & Mon

Alhambra Palace Hotel (£££)
Come here for an early evening drink and enjoy stunning views from the terrace.
✉ Calle Peña 2 ☎ 958 22 14 68

Sevilla (££)
Old haunt of García Lorca and Manuel de Falla. Attractive dining rooms, open air terrace. Good *tapas* bar.
✉ Oficios 12 ☎ 958 22 12 23 🕒 Lunch and dinner, closed Sun

Málaga
Antonio Martin (£££)
Seafront restaurant with large terrace. Long-time favourite specialising in seafood.
✉ Paseo Marítimo ☎ 952 22 21 13 🕒 Lunch and dinner

Café de París (£££)
Elegant restaurant, known for its quality of food and service.
✉ Calle Vélez Málage ☎ 952 22 50 43 🕒 Lunch and dinner, closed Tue

La Cancela (£)
Two small dining rooms. Specialities include *fritura malagueña* and *ajo blanco*.
✉ Calle Denis Belgrano 3 ☎ 952 22 31 25 🕒 Lunch and dinner, closed Wed evening

Tapas
Tapas bars are a way of life in Spain and a visit to some of these establishments in the old part of Málaga will serve to give a feel of the town. A lively atmosphere is usually provided by local people, who meet regularly for animated conversation over a beer or a chilled *fino* sherry. The choice of *tapas* can range from olives, almonds, *jamón serrano* (cured ham), to *tortilla* slices (Spanish-style omelettes), vegetable dishes, and a selection of fish and seafood dishes, often well laced with garlic.

Porciones denote smaller helpings, while *raciones* are more ample. The bars are open for most of the day to serve drinks and food.

93

Budget Food

For inexpensive eating and an informal atmosphere, the coast offers a variety of options. In addition to the famous *tapas* bars, there are *bodegas*, *tabernas* and *cervecerías*, all of which are basically bars which serve food as well. Then there are the popular *chiringuitos*, casual open air beach bar/restaurants, found the length of the coast. A *marisquería* is a restaurant which specialises in seafood, while an *asado* offers barbecued food, usually meats.

Casa del Guardia

One of Málaga's oldest bars, lined with barrels. A good place to sample some of Málaga's sweet wines and great variety of *tapas*.
⊠ **Alameda Principal**
☏ **None** 🕐 **Lunch and dinner**

El Chinitas (££)

Lively, known for its good *tapas*. Specialises in Mediterranean and Andalucían dishes. Commemorative plaques to García Lorca outside.
⊠ **Calle Moreno Monroy 4-6**
☏ **952 21 0972** 🕐 **Lunch and dinner**

La Espuela (££)

Good local dishes in cosy, Andalucían atmosphere.
⊠ **Calle Trinidad** ☏ **952 21 71 82** 🕐 **Lunch and dinner, closed Sun**

El Figón de Bonilla (££)

Known for its good local cooking and fish dishes.
⊠ **Calle Cervantes** ☏ **952 22 32 23** 🕐 **Lunch and dinner, closed Sun**

Lo Güeno (£)

Typical *tapas* bar offering a wide choice. Known for its excellent ham.
⊠ **Calle Maria García** ☏ **952 22 30 12** 🕐 **Lunch and dinner**

Huesca (£)

Pleasant cosy atmosphere.
⊠ **Virgen de la Esperanza 21**
☏ **952 27 55 59** 🕐 **Lunch and dinner, closed Sun & Aug**

Mesón Astorga (££)

Known for its traditional Andalucían cooking.
⊠ **Calle Gerona 11** ☏ **952 34 68 32** 🕐 **Lunch and dinner, closed Wed**

Orellana (££)

Great favourite with Malagueñians. Speciality – stuffed squid.
⊠ **Calle Moreno** ☏ **None** 🕐 **Lunch and dinner**

Refectorium (£££)

Traditional restaurant specialising in meat dishes.
⊠ **Calle Cervantes, 8**
☏ **952 21 89 90** 🕐 **Lunch and dinner**

Rincón de Mata (££)

Well known for its excellent *tapas*. Good value all round.
⊠ **Valle Esparteros** ☏ **952 22 31 35** 🕐 **Lunch and dinner**

La Taberna del Pintor (£)

Specialises in charcoal grilled meat. Informal, appeals to a younger crowd.
⊠ **Calle Maestranza 6**
☏ **952 21 53 15** 🕐 **Lunch and dinner, closed Sun**

Marbella

Bodega Puente Ronda (££)

Tapas served downstairs – cheese and ham served with sherry from the barrel. Formal dining room above known for grilled meat and *paella*.
⊠ **Plaza Puente Ronda 2**
☏ **952 52 00 33**

El Corzo Grill (£££)

In one of the Costa del Sol's top hotels with a restaurant considered one of the best in the region.
⊠ **Los Monteros, Carretera N230** ☏ **952 77 17 00**
🕐 **Lunch and dinner**

La Famiglia (££)

Pleasant little restaurant in the centre of town with Italian pastas and pizzas.
⊠ **Calle Cruz 5 (Plaza Puente Ronda)** ☏ **None** 🕐 **Lunch and dinner, closed Sun**

La Fonda (£££)

Housed in beautiful 18th-century mansion with antique furniture and a lovely patio. International cuisine.

✉ Plaza del Santo Cristo 9
☎ 952 77 25 12 🕐 Dinner only, closed Sun

Gran Marisquería Santiago (££)

Good seafood restaurant on the seafront, favoured by locals.

✉ Duque de Ahumada
☎ 952 77 00 78 🕐 Lunch and dinner

La Hacienda (£££)

Top restaurant with reputation for *haute cuisine*. Good location up hill with sea views.

✉ Urbanización Las Chapas, N340 (12km east of Marbella)
☎ 952 83 12 67 🕐 Dinner only in summer; closed Mon, Tue and mid-Nov to mid-Dec

Marbella Club (£££)

Top quality restaurant in Marbella's famous hotel.

✉ Carretera N340 (west of Málaga) ☎ 952 77 13 00
🕐 Lunch and dinner

La Pesquera (££)

Located in tiny square in town. Bar and restaurant serving good seafood.

✉ Plaza de la Victoria ☎ 952 86 14 04 🕐 Lunch and dinner

Mijas

El Padtrasto (£££)

Spectacular situation on clifftop with good views from the terrace of Fuengirola and the coast. Local specialities and international cooking.

✉ Paseo del Compás
☎ 952 48 51 97 🕐 Lunch and dinner

Mirlo Blanco (££)

Basque cuisine, good fish dishes.

✉ Paseo del Compás
☎ 952 48 57 00 🕐 Lunch and dinner

Valparaíso (££)

Valparaíso is housed in an attractively situated villa with gardens and pool. There is a terrace, and dancing in the evening.

✉ Carretera de Mijas km 4
☎ 952 48 59 96 🕐 Dinner only; closed Sun

Nerja

Cielito Lindo (££)

Cielito Lindo is converted into a Mexican-style restaurant with a selection of Mexican dishes on offer, or choose from a selection of charcoal grilled meats.

✉ Calle El Barrio ☎ 952 52 36 21 🕐 Lunch, dinner. Closed Nov

Mesón Antonio (£)

Good value *tapas* bar offering wide range of dishes.

✉ Calle Diputación 18 ☎ 952 52 00 33 🕐 Lunch and dinner. Closed Wed

Nueva Andalucía

Casa Italia (££)

Italian and international cuisine served in a friendly and lively ambience.

✉ Calle 17B (behind Hotel Andalucía Plaza) ☎ 952 81 73 17 🕐 Lunch, dinner daily

Restaurante Vienna (££)

New restaurant with traditional Austrian dishes. Excellent stone-grilled fillet of pork. Warm, welcoming atmosphere.

✉ Plaza de las Orquideas, Calle 2B ☎ 952 81 28 71
🕐 Lunch, dinner. Closed Sun

What to Drink

Wine is widely drunk with meals, with a preference for red wine, sometimes taken chilled. White and rosé wines are also available and a pleasant alternative is a jug of *sangría*. Based on a combination of red wine, fruit and a liqueur, topped up with lemonade and ice, this is best enjoyed when eating out in the open air on a warm sunny day. Spain has excellent beer, fruit juices and soft drinks. An acquired taste is *Horchata*, a nonalcoholic drink based on almonds and barley.

For afters, there is a wide range of *coñacs* (Spanish brandy) ranging from the inexpensive Fundador or Terry, to the special savour of a Carlos I.

Healthy Ingredients

Olives have been cultivated since the time of the Greeks and Andalucía produces one of the most important olive crops in the world. The production of olive oil involves arduous work, from the collection of the crops towards December, to the first pressing, which is known as virgin oil. Olive oil forms an integral part of Spanish cooking and scientific research suggests it is good for the health, as is garlic, which also features widely in Spanish cuisine.

Eat Spanish

Restaurants should always offer a *menu del día* (menu of the day) which includes a three-course meal and a drink. These are usually very reasonable in price and can be good value. Real local cooking is more likely to be found in smaller restaurants or away from the coast and tourist areas.

In line with much of the country, the Spaniards tend to eat late: lunch is normally taken from about 2PM and can well carry on to early evening! Many diners will arrive around 10PM or so. The trendier the place, the later the action.

Many restaurants are closed one day a week, but the day varies from one to another, so check beforehand.

Puerto Banús

Azul Marino (££)
Brasserie-restaurant, good for fish and seafood.
🖂 Front Line, Port I ☎ 952 81 10 44 🕐 Lunch and dinner

Christian Bistro du Port (££)
One of Puerto Banús's earliest restaurants, ever popular.
🖂 In the port ☎ 952 81 10 06 🕐 Lunch and dinner

Dalli's Pizza Factory (££)
Lively place for a rendezvous. Typical Italian dishes and new dishes with a difference. Fresh pasta and pizza dishes also available to take away.
🖂 Puerto Banús Marina ☎ 952 81 86 23 🕐 Lunch, dinner

Don Leone (£££)
Longtime favourite, open air, overlooking marina. Mainly Italian cuisine.
🖂 Muelle Ribera ☎ 952 81 17 16 🕐 Lunch and dinner; closed end-Nov–end-Dec

Fleming's Grill (££)
Homely interior, relaxed atmosphere. Specialises in large succulent grilled steaks.
🖂 Benabola Complex ☎ 952 81 76 94 🕐 Lunch, dinner

Restaurante Cipriano (£££)
Highly acclaimed seafood restaurant. Stylish décor with attractively covered terrace. Boasts a regular clientèle.
🖂 Avenida Playas del Duque, Edificio Sevilla ☎ 952 81 10 77 🕐 Lunch, dinner

La Taberna del Alabardero (£££)
High class restaurant. Specialises in Spanish, Basque and international cuisine.
🖂 Muelle Benabola ☎ 952 81 27 94 🕐 Lunch and dinner; closed mid-Jan–Feb

San Pedro de Alcántara

Destille Brandenburg (££)
German restaurant offering traditional fare such as potato soup and *eisbein* (knuckle of pork).
🖂 Avenida Oriental 7 (near the church) ☎ 952 78 72 53 🕐 Lunch, dinner. Closed Tue and Aug

La Estrella (£££)
Lively atmosphere, popular with the Spanish crowd. Known for its good selection of fish dishes.
🖂 Avenida Andalucia, Local 10 ☎ 952 78 34 06 🕐 Lunch, dinner. Closed Tue

San Roque

Los Remos (£££)
High class restaurant housed in neoclassical villa with attractive gardens. Known for good fish and seafood dishes.
🖂 Villa Victoria S, Campamento ☎ 956 10 68 12 🕐 Lunch and dinner, closed Sun

Sevilla

Enrique Becerra (££)
Small, lively establishment, centrally located. Popular bar, attractively tiled. Good traditional dishes served.
🖂 Calle Gamazo 2 ☎ 954 21 30 49 🕐 Lunch, dinner. Closed Sun

Girarda (£)
Tiny place set in attractive patio, right in the heart of the picturesque Barrio de Santa Cruz. Spanish cuisine.
🖂 Calle Justino de Neve 8 ☎ 954 21 51 13 🕐 Lunch, dinner

La Albahaca (££)

Housed in a typical Andalucían house, attractively decorated with tiles and plants. Spanish and French cuisine.

✉ Plaza Santa Cruz ☎ 954 22 07 14 🕐 Lunch and dinner, closed Sun

Mesón Don Raimundo (££)

Mesón Don Raimundo is a small, cosy restaurant with ceramic tiles. It specialises in meat dishes.

✉ Argote de Molina 26 ☎ 954 22 33 55 🕐 Lunch and dinner; closed Sun evening

Sotogrande
Le Bistro (££)

Popular for salads and light dishes. Daily specials on the menu.

✉ Galerías Paniagua ☎ 956 79 59 42 🕐 Lunch, dinner. Closed Sun

Midas (££)

Attractive setting in the port. Known for its excellent meat dishes. Fondues and homemade desserts are a speciality.

✉ Puerto Sotogrande ☎ 956 79 02 42 🕐 Lunch, dinner

Torremolinos
El Atrio (££)

El Atrio is a cosy restaurant with a pleasant atmosphere and French menu.

✉ Casablanca 9, Plaza Pueblo Blanco ☎ 952 38 88 50 🕐 Dinner only, closed Sun and Dec

El Bodegón (££)

Cosy atmosphere, centrally located, dishes to suit all tastes.

✉ Calle 4 ☎ 952 38 20 12 🕐 Lunch and dinner

Casa Juan (£)

Good reputation for fresh seafood. Patio overlooking the sea.

✉ Paseo Marítimo 29, La Carihuela ☎ 952 37 65 23 🕐 Dinner only, closed Mon

El Comedor (££)

El Comedor is an elegant establishment in the centre of town. Mainly Basque cuisine, with a regular change of menu.

✉ Calle Pueblo Blanco ☎ 952 38 38 81 🕐 Lunch, dinner

Hawaii (££)

Worth making your way up through this complex for the panoramic view of old Torremolinos and the bay, best from the open air terrace. German run, friendly service.

✉ Centro Comercial Balcón San Miguel ☎ 952 38 51 97 🕐 Lunch and dinner

Mesón Galego Antoxo (££)

Attractive rustic setting for meat and fish dishes from Galicia.

✉ Calle Hoyo 5 ☎ 952 38 45 33 🕐 Lunch and dinner

La Paella (££)

La Paella is a long-established beachside restaurant, known for serving good paella. Meat and fish and a selection of Spanish dishes are also on the menu.

✉ Playa Bajondillo ☎ 952 37 50 55 🕐 Lunch, dinner

El Roqueo (££)

Favourite with the locals. Good reputation for fresh fish.

✉ Carmen 35, La Carihuela ☎ 952 38 49 46 🕐 Lunch and dinner, closed Tue and Nov

Local Delicacies

A popular starter is the Andalucían speciality, *gaspacho Andaluz*, a chilled tomato soup with additions, although this is not always on the menu in winter. Other favourites are asparagus, *jamón serrano* (cured ham), *entremés de carne* (cold meats), tuna salad, *calamares a la romana* (fried squid rings).

For the main course there is often a good selection of fish dishes, although they can be pricey. *Fritura Malagueña* (an assortment of fried fish) and fish baked in salt, are specialities, while you can always ask for the catch of the day. Otherwise pork, chicken and rabbit, grilled (*a la plancha*) or prepared with a sauce, are usually a good bet. There is always *paella*, which can be taken as a first or main course.

Desserts tend to be limited, with *flan* (*crème caramel*), ice cream or fresh fruit of the season among the most popular choices.

Hotels in Costa del Sol & Beyond

Prices
Prices are for a double room, excluding breakfast and VAT:

£ = under 11,000 pesetas
££ = 11,000–22,000 pesetas
£££ = over 22,000 pesetas

Hotel Gradings
Officially registered hotels in Spain range from 1 to 5 star (with an additional top deluxe category of GL, Gran Lujo). Other types of accommodation include apartment hotels, hotel residencias (no restaurant), hostels and pensions. Stars are assigned according to services and facilities available. Suites can usually be found in the 4 or 5-star range. Tariffs should be displayed.

Antequera
Parador de Antequera (£)
Modern building in attractive setting amongst ruins of the Moorish fortress.
✉ García de Olmo s/n
☎ 952 84 02 61

Benalmádena Costa
Las Arenas (£)
Six-floor hotel situated opposite the Arroyo de la Miel and Bil Bil Castle beaches. Most rooms with sea views and terrace; pool, garden, table tennis.
✉ Ctra de Cádiz, Km 221
☎ 952 44 36 44

Torrequebrada (£££)
Top deluxe hotel with sports facilities.
✉ Carretera de Cádiz, Km 220
☎ 952 44 60 00

Triton (££)
Long established hotel set in sub-tropical gardens, with mountain and sea views. Facilities include swimming pools, 2 floodlit tennis courts, golf club near by.
✉ Avenida Antonio Machado 29 ☎ 952 44 26 49

Córdoba
Hotel Residencia Marisa (£)
Modest, no restaurant. Central location right by the mosque.
✉ Cardenal Herrero 6 ☎ 957 47 31 42

Melía Córdoba (££)
Pleasant and centrally located.
✉ Jardines de la Victoria
☎ 957 29 80 66

Estepona
Atalaya Park (£)
Comfortable, set in attractive gardens facing the beach with sports facilities.
✉ Carretera N340 ☎ 952 88 48 01

Beach Hotel Las Dunas (£££)
Luxurious hotel on the beach, located between Marbella and Estepona. Attractive scenery, tropical gardens, Andalucían style décor with a Middle Eastern influence. Swimming pool, gourmet restaurant, watersports, riding and clinic for therapeutic and beauty treatments.
✉ La Boladilla Baja, Ctra de Cádiz, Km 163.5 ☎ 952 79 43 45

Caracas (£)
Small hotel situated in a quiet area near the centre of town and some 100m from the beach. Spacious restaurant-bar.
✉ Avenida San Lorenzo 32
☎ 952 80 08 00

Hotel El Paraiso (££)
Set on a hill with good views of the coast and attractive gardens with waterfalls, surrounded by a golf course. Large outdoor and heated pool, riding.
✉ Ctra de Cádiz, Km 134
☎ 952 88 30 00

Santa Marta (£)
Attractive little Andalucían style hotel with bungalows, situated on the seafront. Shady gardens and pool with bar.
✉ Ctra de Cádiz, Km 167
☎ 952 88 81 77

Fuengirola
Angela (£)
Attractively decorated in a modern Andalucían style, the hotel is one of many located on the Paseo Marítimo,

within walking distance of the beach. Shops, rail and bus transport are all near by.

✉ **Paseo Marítimo, s/n**
☎ **952 47 61 00**

Florida (££)

One of Fuengirola's earliest establishments, the hotel has a swimming pool set in semitropical gardens, with live music and shows during the summer.

✉ **Paseo Marítimo, s/n**
☎ **952 47 61 00**

Las Palmeras (££)

Comfortable. Located on the seafront.

✉ **Paseo Marítimo** ☎ **952 47 27 00**

Las Pirámides (££)

This hotel is situated on the Paseo Marítimo, near the beach and the town centre. Facilities include a garden and pool, flamenco shows and live music. Golf, mini golf and tennis near by.

✉ **Miquel Márquez, 43**
☎ **952 47 06 00**

Stella Maris (£)

Old time favourite which commands a good position on the promenade in a residential area. Close to the beach and some 10 minutes from the town centre. Swimming pool, riding, golf and tennis.

✉ **Paseo Marítimo** ☎ **952 47 54 50**

Granada
Alhambra Palace (££)

Old traditional favourite with Moorish-style décor. Close to the Alhambra with views of the Sierra Nevada from some rooms.

✉ **Calle Peña Partida, 2**
☎ **(958) 22 14 68**

Dauro II (£)

Modest and centrally located in small pedestrianised street. Bar and coffee shop.

✉ **Navas 5** ☎ **958 22 15 81**

Málaga
Hotel Residencia Los Naranjos (£)

In residential district, near the centre. Small garden with orange trees.

✉ **Paseo Sancha, 35** ☎ **952 22 43 17**

Parador Málaga-Gibralfaro (££)

Attractively situated high up the hill by Gibralfaro Castle with magnificent views of Málaga and bay.

✉ **Gibralfaro**
☎ **952 22 19 02**

Marbella
Andalucía Plaza (££)

Spacious establishment, attractively refurbished, set in gardens, two pools, casino.

✉ **Nueva Andalucia (opposite Puerto Banús)** ☎ **952 81 20 00**

Coral Beach (££)

New hotel situated on the seafront beside Puerto Banús within the famous Golden Mile. It offers two swimming pools, sauna, jacuzzi, gymnasium. Golf, watersports and casino in the vicinity.

✉ **Ctra de Cádiz, Km 176**
☎ **952 82 45 00**

Don Carlos (£££)

One of the area's top deluxe hotels.

✉ **Ctra de Cádiz** ☎ **952 83 11 40**

El Fuerte (££)

Attractive hotel set in pleasant gardens. Excellent location near the sea and

Travellers with Disabilities

Facilities for travellers with disabilities are little evident; however, there are signs of progress in this area. Certain hotels in the region offer fixed and mobile ramps, lifts, and wider doorways, corridors and toilets to accommodate wheelchairs and parking areas close to the hotel entrance. If such services are required, check that the hotel in question carries the wheelchair symbol and state your needs before booking.

For further information on facilities for disabled visitors wishing to visit the area contact:

Las Gerencias Provinciales del Instituto Andaluz de Servicios Sociales (Provincial Management of the Andalucían Institute of Social Services)

✉ Avenida Manuel Agustín 26, 4, Málaga.
☎ (952) 21 04 12/13/14

Paradores

Very pleasant accommodation is provided by the *parador*, originally denoting a lodging place for the gentry. The late 1920s saw the development of this network of state-run establishments. Often in attractively converted old castles and historic buildings, *paradores* are scattered throughout the country, making good stopovers when touring by car. There are also some purpose-built modern *paradores* in tourist centres, many set in tranquil gardens, often with a pool, in lovely surroundings. Although tariffs have risen over the years, the splendour of the buildings and their locations make an overnight stay well worthwhile.

within walking distance of Marbella centre.

✉ **Avenida El Fuerte** ☎ **952 86 15 00**

Grand Meliá Don Pepe (£££)

Super deluxe hotel with gardens, pools.

✉ **José Meliá DP** ☎ **952 77 03 00**

Las Chapas (£)

Set in lovely pine groves, this is an old time favourite, popular with families, sports and nature lovers. Tennis, mini golf, table tennis offered, with riding, golf and watersports in the locale.

✉ **Ctra de Cádiz, Km 198** ☎ **952 83 13 75**

Marbella Club (££)

Old time favourite. Bungalow-style rooms. Set in lush gardens with swimming pool.

✉ **Blvd Príncipe Alfonso de Hohenlohe** ☎ **952 82 22 11**

Los Monteros (£££)

One of the Costa del Sol's top hotels. Pool, golf course, sports facilities.

✉ **Carretera Cádiz, Km 187** ☎ **952 77 17 00**

Puente Romano (£££)

Super deluxe village-like complex with landscaped gardens, pool, tennis.

✉ **Carretera N340, between Marbella and Puerto Banús** ☎ **952 82 09 00**

San Cristobal (£)

Modest, conveniently situated for Marbella centre.

✉ **Ramon y Cajal 3** ☎ **952 77 12 50**

Mijas

Byblos Andaluz (£££)

Super deluxe hotel set in

attractive gardens.

✉ **Urbanización Mijas-Golf** ☎ **952 46 02 50**

Hotel Mijas (£)

Located at the entrance to Mijas, the hotel is set amidst gardens with a pool, offering superb views down to the coast.

✉ **Urb Tamisa s/n** ☎ **952 48 58 00**

Monda

Castillo de Monda (££)

Old castle recently converted into a hotel by British proprietors. Moorish style furnishings, stunning views of Monda village and landscapes of the Sierra de las Nieves.

✉ **Monda (18km northeast of Marbella)** ☎ **952 45 71 42**

Nerja

Balcón de Europa (££)

Old favourite located on the promenade of the same name. Private beach.

✉ **Paseo Balcón de Europa** ☎ **952 52 08 00**

Parador de Nerja (££)

Modern *parador* set high up with pleasant gardens. Splendid views of the beach below and surrounding bay.

✉ **Almuñécar 8** ☎ **952 52 00 50**

Villa Flamenca (£)

Situated in the Nueva Nerja development some 300m from the beach, the hotel has a garden and swimming pool, restaurant and bar.

✉ **Urb. Nueva Nerja** ☎ **952 52 32 00**

Rincón de la Victoria

Hotel Elimar (£)

Located about 10 minutes from Málaga by road, the

hotel has an attractive position overlooking the sea. Amenities include an open air terrace with live music and a large gymnasium with good equipment for body building and keep fit enthusiasts.

✉ **Avenida del Mediterráneo 230** ☎ 952 40 12 27

Ronda
Reina Victoria (££)
Another old favourite, built by the British at the beginning of the century. Set in attractive gardens with swimming pool. Fine views of surrounding mountains.

✉ **Calle Jerez 25** ☎ 952 87 12 40

San Pedro de Alcántara
Golf Hotel Guadalmina (££)
Long established favourite of golfers. Located by the sea and set in attractive grounds – surrounded by golf courses

✉ **Hacienda Guadalmina**
☎ 952 88 22 11

Sevilla
Alfonso XIII (£££)
One of Spain's most famous hotels. Built around a large courtyard with arches and plenty of greenery. Unique décor in Moorish style with magnificent marble floors, panelled ceilings and beautiful ceramic tiles. Gardens and swimming pool.

✉ **Calle San Fernando 2**
☎ 954 22 28 50

Bécquer (£)
Pleasant establishment. Good location, short distance from the town centre and the river.

✉ **Calle Reyes Católicos 4**
☎ 954 22 89 00

Residencia Murillo (£)
Modest, comfortable. Located in the heart of the Barrio Santa Cruz.

✉ **Lope de Rueda 7**
☎ 954 21 60 95

Torremolinos
Al-Andalus (££)
Situated in the Montemar area, near La Carihuela beach, the hotel has a swimming pool set in gardens and offers tennis, table tennis and a varied programme of entertainments.

✉ **Calle Al-Andalus 3**
☎ 952 38 12 00

Cervantes (££)
Large hotel a few minutes' walk from town centre. Garden with pool, rooftop pool, restaurant and casino. Live music and dancing.

✉ **Calle Las Mercedes s/n**
☎ 952 38 40 33

Fénix (£)
Situated right in the centre of Torremolinos, with direct access to the beach. Swimming pool set in a garden, sauna, gymnasium and evening entertainment.

✉ **Las Mercedes 24** ☎ 952 37 52 68

Meliá Costa del Sol (££)
Excellent position on El Bajondillo beach. Wide range of entertainments available, including chess, cards, bingo, table tennis, flamenco shows. Gardens, pool.

✉ **Paseo Marítimo, Playa del Bajondillo** ☎ 952 38 66 77

Meliá Torremolinos (£££)
Luxury hotel with tropical gardens, pool.

✉ **Avenida Carlota Alessandri 109** ☎ 952 38 05 00

Rural Retreats
As a total contrast to the beach, visitors may like to venture into Andalucía's hinterland. At a short distance from the coast are to be found a number of so-called rural lodgings, which can vary from country cottages, rooms in attractive *haciendas* to mountain refuges or hostels and facilities for camping. In addition to wonderful scenery and fresh mountain air, there are often possibilities for hiking, riding and other pursuits.

Information and Reservation Centre:
✉ R.A.A.R. (Red Andaluza de Alojamientos Rurales) Apdo. 2035, 04080 Almería
☎ 951 26 50 18

Shopping in Costa del Sol & Beyond

Shopping in Málaga
The most concentrated shopping area in Málaga is in and around calle Marqués de Larios, north of the Alameda Principal, Málaga's main boulevard. Within easy walking distance are a host of shops and boutiques which stock a variety of goods, geared more to local needs than to visiting tourists.

If you take time to browse around, however, you will come across some very attractive ceramics and handicrafts, antiques, leather goods (shoes can be a good buy) and jewellery, in addition to the odd souvenir and gift shop.

Anticuarios (Antique Shops)

Málaga
A Ruiz Linares
✉ Avenida Comte Benítez 7
☎ 952 22 35 00

A Vela Díaz
✉ San Augustín ☎ 952 21 20 02

El Martinete
✉ Carretería 90 ☎ 952 21 33 35

El Trianon
✉ Madre de Dios 22 ☎ 952 21 08 46

Nueva Andalucía
Anticuariato
Paintings and antiques, including Spanish and international works. Auctions are held in adjacent premises on Sat at noon.
✉ Centro Plaza 22 ☎ 952 81 41 11

Ronda
El Portón
✉ Manuel Montero 14
☎ 952 87 14 69

Muñoz Soto
✉ B S Juan de Dios de Córdoba 34 ☎ 952 87 14 51

Bookstores

Nerja
Nerja Book Centre
Large secondhand book store, stocking thousands of books in various languages.
✉ Calle Granda 30 ☎ 952 52 09 08

Boutiques

Fuengirola
Brandtex
Ladies' boutique with stylish fashionware available in all sizes. Good selection of mix and match outfits.
✉ Avenida Suel 4, Edificio Tres Coronas ☎ 952 58 25 85

Málaga
Lorem's Boutique
Specialists in blouses, in cotton and man-made fibres.
✉ Sancha de Lara 13 ☎ 952 21 57 35

Vogue Costura
One of Málaga's top fashion shops, stocking famous brand names.
✉ Sancha de Lara 6 ☎ 952 21 56 16

Marbella
Don Miguel
Long established, with wide range of fashionwear for men and women. Some of the brand names to be found here.
✉ Avenida Ricardo Soriano 5
☎ 952 77 31 40

Louis Feraud
Fashion clothes by Feraud, known for their striking designs and vibrant colours.
✉ Plaza Victoria ☎ 952 82 81 06

Nara Camice
This boutique stocks beautifully embroidered cotton blouses suitable for both casual and formal occasions, ranging from intricate to simple, elegant designs.
✉ Calle Penal 19 ☎ 952 82 53 19

Scampi
Specialises in Swedish designed swim and gym ware.
✉ Calle Nueva 11, near Plaza de los Naranjos (Orange Square)

☎ 952 86 28 84

Nerja

Bruna Cavvalini

Some good bargains may be had in this fashionable ladies' boutique. Sportswear and more formal gear available, plus accessories. Clothes from Sevilla and London.

✉ **Calle Barrio**
☎ 952 52 30 58

Mostaza

Mainly for men. Casual and formal wear. Good for shirts and sweaters, suits and jackets.

✉ **Calle Diputación Provincial 6** ☎ **952 52 14 00**

Puerto Banús

Boutique Donna Piu

Italian-style fashion.

✉ **Benabola** ☎ **952 81 49 90**

Boutique Number One

Specialises in French and Italian designer collections.

✉ **Levante 1** ☎ **952 81 16 97**

Torre del Mar

Singh

Elegant boutique for women's and men's clothes. Top fashion names, with the latest designs.

✉ **Calle Avenida de Andalucía 121** ☎ **952 54 10 91**

Ceramics

Estepona

Cerámica La Chiminea

Beautiful designs created by Paco Leonicio, who learnt his crafts from masters at Triana, one of Spain's top centres for pottery. Wide selection available of decorative tiles, glazed and unglazed ceramics.

✉ **Polígono Industrial, Calle El Cerillo 6** ☎ **952 79 44 75**

Málaga

Cerámica Fina

Cerámica Fina stocks attractively displayed ceramics of all kinds showing a high standard of workmanship. Ideal for gifts.

✉ **Calle Coronel 5, near the church of San Juan** ☎ **No phone available**

San Pedro de Alcántara

Artesanía Troyano

Specialists in porcelain, features Lladró porcelain and other fine makes.

✉ **Calle Lagasca 63. Also in Marqués del Duero** ☎ **952 78 11 99**

Sevilla

Sevillarte

A wide range of beautiful ceramic products at three different branches.

✉ **Branches at: Gloria 5**
☎ **954 21 88 35; Sierpes 66**
☎ **954 21 28 36; Vida 13**
☎ **954 56 29 45**

Food and Wine Shops

Puerto Banús

Club de Gourmet

Exciting range of unusual and 'exotic' products, definitely aimed at gourmet visitors. Bar Inglés, cafetería and restaurant adjoining.

✉ **By entrance to Puerto Banús, near El Corte Inglés**
☎ **952 81 78 00**

Benalmádena

BRC Hipermarket

Huge selection of food, wines and spirits, in addition to good value household goods.

✉ **Avenida Salvador Vicente 2, Arroyo de la Miel** ☎ **952 44 58 39**

Puerto Banús

Puerto Banús is a very different shopping scene. These former orange-growing farmlands were developed in the sixties by the businessman Don José Banús to become the successful international centre it is today.
For those who like to shop at trendy boutiques stocked with designer goods, against the glamorous background of yachts and a chic ambience, Puerto Banús is a veritable mecca – at a price!

Department Stores

The mammoth department store has become a sign of the times in Spain and an increasing number are to be found on the Costa del Sol. El Corte Inglés is a household name in Spain. It started trading way back in 1939, selling only English fabric. Over the years the group has expanded into a large chain of stores located all over Spain and selling an increasing range of items 'made in Spain'.

One of the newest is within the new Costa Marbella Commercial Centre located by the entrance to Puerto Banús. Combined with the Hipercor supermarket the complex offers an enormous range of goods under one roof.

Marbella
BRC Hipermarket
(See above)
✉ Ctra de Cádiz km 179
☎ 952 77 59 29

Gift Shops

Benalmádena (Puerto Marina)
La Maison
Variety of small gifts such as porcelain items and ceramic fish.
✉ Puerto Marina ☎ 952 56 0299

Fuengirola
Regalos de Arte Maxi
Attractive choice of Lladró porcelain, ceramics from Sevilla, Majorcan pearls and a good selection of easy to carry gifts.
✉ Ramón y Cajal 1 ☎ 952 47 33 34

Málaga
Original
A variety of gifts made in wood, including reproductions of music boxes and antique toys.
✉ Calle Caldería 2, and Calle Marín García 6 ☎ None

Nueva Andalucía
Decoraciones Los Portales
Attractive gifts for the home, including glassware and placemats.
✉ Centro Plaza, Locales 16–17
☎ 952 81 88 20

Torremolinos
Las Tres Torres
Good choice of products, including a wide range of items made in Toledo steel, ceramics from Sevilla and attractive selection of Majorcan pearls.
✉ Calle San Miguel 17
☎ 952 21 79 39

Montinas Gift Shop
A wide variety of attractive gifts available. Official agents for Lladró, Majorica and Swarovski.
✉ La Nogalera, 26 ☎ 952 38 11 78

Regalos Geni
Wide range of gifts, including good selection of Lladró, Swarovski crystal and Joseph Bofill sculpture.
✉ Calle San Miguel 8
☎ 952 38 28 05

Jewellery

Fuengirola
Nicholson
Specialises in modern jewellery designs; selection of earrings, bracelets, pendants and other items. Another shop in Marbella's Orange Square.
✉ Calle Marbella s/n
☎ 952 47 58 82

Marbella
Cendra
Stocks unusual jewellery, with an emphasis on earrings, rings and pillboxes. Selection of attractive amber pieces and some porcelain.
✉ Avenida Arias Maldonada 5
☎ 952 82 04 43

San Pedro de Alcántara
Anthony's Jewellers
Unusual and original designs by the owner, with many pieces incorporating semi-precious stones.
✉ Plaza las Faroles ☎ 952 78 62 74

Torremolinos
Joyería Crystal
Good for gold and diamond jewellery and watches, in addition to Lladró porcelain

and cultured pearls.

 Calle San Miguel 45

☎ 952 37 50 51

Leatherware

Benalmádena

Artesanía Piel

Leather goods produced on the premises. Out of the ordinary belts and handicrafts.

✉ Puerto Marina ☎ No phone

Fuengirola

Bravo

Good reputation for shoes, handbags, luggage and leather accessories. Shops also in Marbella and Torremolinos.

✉ Avenida Condes de San Isidro 33 ☎ 952 46 17 19

Málaga

Nuñez Antilope

Nuñez Antilope is an old leather factory stocking suede and leather gear.

✉ Bolsa s/n ☎ 952 21 27 45

Rosselli

Good selection of leather shoes and bags, for women and men.

✉ Calle Molino Larios

☎ 952 21 43 23

Marbella

Charles Jourdan

Wide range of shoes and leather goods, well displayed. Other items include jewellery, umbrellas and sun glasses.

✉ Avenida Ramón y Cajal

☎ 952 77 00 03

Torremolinos

Zerimar

Specialises in handbags, traditional leather goods and raw silk outfits.

✉ Calle San Miguel ☎ None

Stores

Málaga

El Corte Inglés

Six floors of fashion, gifts, exhibitions of arts and crafts.

✉ Avenida de Andalucia 4–6

☎ 952 30 00 00

Felix Saenz

Málaga's first department store. Wide range of goods available from inexpensive to sophisticated brand names.

✉ Felix Saenz Plaza s/n

☎ 952 22 56 00

Málaga Plaza Centro Comercial

American-style complex with a variety of quality shops.

✉ Armengual de la Mota 12

☎ 952 61 40 40

Rosaleda

A light, spacious centre with over 100 shops including a bookstore, hairdressers, a supermarket, various interior furnishing shops, 14 cinema screens and a video club. Several casual restaurants withing the complex add to the enjoyment of shopping.

✉ Centro Rosaleda, Avenida Simon Bolivar ☎ 952 88 05 00

Puerto Banús

Centro Plaza

Another gigantic shopping complex with a crystal shop, bank, hairdresser, and restaurants.

✉ Opposite Puerto Banús, past the bullring

El Corte Inglés

This new superstore, at the entrance to Puerto Banús, has an enormous variety of quality goods under one roof.

✉ Centro Commercial Costa Marbella ☎ 952 81 78 00

Markets

Street markets in Spain are great fun to visit. Major centres along the coast have a weekly market, generally open from early in the morning to around 2:30PM.

Attractive displays of fruit and vegetables create a profusion of colour. In addition to enjoying the lively ambience of clamour and bustling activity, there is always the chance of picking up a bargain. Popular items for bringing back as gifts include pottery and ceramics, leatherware, straw baskets, hats and the occasional piece of costume jewellery.

Children's Activities

Fun for Kids

Spaniards are known for their fondness for children, who can expect to be treated with courtesy and made to feel welcome.

There is plenty to amuse youngsters down on the Costa. Apart from the obvious pleasures of the beach or pool, which may suffice for some, the area has many attractions aimed at entertaining young visitors of all ages. Amusement and aqua parks offer all kinds of entertainment such as water slides, kamikaze rapids and wave pools. Some aqua parks are closed in the winter, so check this out.

The Sea Life Centre at Benalmádena's Marina, demonstrations of birds of prey, the zoo at Fuengirola and fun rides in mini trains around some of the main centres are also worth considering.

Children are also sure to enjoy the fun and colour of a local fiesta, should the opportunity arise.

Benalmádena
Tivoli World, Arroyo de la Miel

This show and amusement park, set in extensive grounds, is a great favourite with families, especially at the weekend. In addition to numerous rides and amusements for the children (including a giant rollercoaster), visitors can enjoy flamenco shows, a Wild West Town, theatre and live music.

✉ **Ctra de Benalmádena, Arroyo de la Miel** ☎ **952 57 70 16** 🕐 **Daily May, Sep 4PM–1AM; Jun 5PM–2AM; Jul, Aug 6PM–3AM; Oct, Nov, Mar, Apr 1PM–12 midnight; Dec, Jan, Feb 1PM–10PM** 🍴 **Restaurants (£–££)** 🚉 **RENFE station Banalmádena or Arroyo de la Miel** ♿ **Few** 💵 **Moderate**

Benalmádena Costa
Sea Life Parque Submarino

This sea life centre takes you on an exciting voyage of discovery to the bottom of the ocean. From the shallow waters to the depths of the sea you can enjoy close views of a whole wealth of marine life, ranging from tiny shrimps and starfish to giant stingrays and great sharks. There are also presentations and feeding displays.

✉ **Puerto Deportivo, Benalmádena** ☎ **952 56 01 50** 🕐 **Year round daily 10–6** 🍴 **Restaurant (££)** 🚉 **RENFE station Benalmádena** ♿ **Good** 💵 **Moderate**

Moncho's Tourist Train

Children may also enjoy a ride in this mini-train which chugs around the marina at regular intervals.

✉ **Puerto Marina, Benalmádena**

Banalmádena Pueblo
Jardín de las Aguílas (Eagle Gardens)

Up the hill, in the Castillo de Aguílas, is the Birds of Prey Centre, where demonstrations are held with eagles, owls, falcons and vultures. Enjoyable for children and nature lovers.

✉ **Castillo de Aguílas just before Benalmádena Pueblo** ☎ **952 56 82 39** 🕐 **Tue–Sun Sep 1–7; Oct, Mar 1–5; Nov, Dec, Jan, Feb 1–4; Apr 1–6:30; May, Jun, Jul, Aug 1–8. Performances take place subject to weather** 🚌 **Bus to Benalmádena Pueblo** ♿ **Good** 💵 **Moderate**

Estepona
Prado World

Popular children's fun fair and water park, located just off the coastal road between Marbella and Estepona. Covering a wide area, the park offers a bewildering variety of amusements, from pools, water chutes and trampolines, to roller skating, mini golf and bumper cars. There is also a picnic area for barbecuing your own food.

✉ **Ctra de Cádiz, between Marbella and Estepona** ☎ **952 79 11 74** 🕐 **Summer daily from 10 onwards; winter Sat–Sun and pub hol from 11** 🚉 **None** 🍴 **None** ♿ **Few** 💵 **Moderate**

Fuengirola
Parquesam Zoo

The Costa del Sol's only zoo is a small one, but it does have a variety of animals, a reptile house, and a children's playground with a mini train.

✉ **Avenida Camilio José Cela s/n** ☎ **952 47 15 90** 🕐 **Daily 10–6 (or according to season)**

🚉 **RENFE station Fuengirola**
♿ **Few** 👍 **Moderate**

Minitrain
This takes off from the port every 30 minutes for a short ride around Fuengirola town.
✉ **Marina, Fuengirola**

Granada
Parque de las Ciencias (Science Park)
This science park has a planetarium and offers much of interest to children who can take part in experiments.
✉ **Avenida del Mediterraneo s/n** ☎ **958 13 19 00**
🕐 **Tue–Sat 10–7, Sun 10–3, closed Mon** 🚉 **RENFE station Granada** ♿ **Few** 👍 **Cheap**

Marbella
Funny Beach Karting
This offers fun for the whole family, with go karts, mini bikes, jet ski and a children's play area.
✉ **Entrance to Marbella, km 184** ☎ **952 82 33 59** 🕐 **Daily 10AM–11PM** 🍴 **Waterski Restaurant (££)** 🚌 **Bus stop Marbella** ♿ **None** 👍 **Moderate**

Mijas Costa
Parque Acuático Mijas (Aqualand)
This water theme park has great watershoots, including a thrilling Kamikaze, pools, slides and rapids.
✉ **Ctra N-340, km 209** ☎ **952 46 04 04** 🕐 **May 10– 5:30; Jun and Sep 10–6; Jul and Aug 10–7; Oct–Apr closed** 🍴 **Restaurant (££)** 🚌 **Fuengirola bus station** ♿ **Few** 👍 **Expensive**

Puerto Banús
Centro de Observación Marina
This marine observatory is the headquarters for rescue and research into marine life in Europe. A wide range of Mediterranean sea creatures is kept here for scientific observation, for rehabilitation or health-checks before being passed on to other oceanariums. Many of the creatures being cared for and observed can also be seen in more natural surroundings, such as the Sea Life Parque Submarino in Puerto Marina, Benalmádena Costa (➤ 106).
✉ **Torre de Control, Puerto Banús, Nueva Andalucía (Marbella)** ☎ **952 81 40 80** 🕐 **Check locally for opening times**

Super Bonanza
The *Bonanza* departs every two hours from midday onwards for a cruise along the coast.
✉ **Sinatra Bar, Puerto Banús** ☎ **952 38 55 00**

Torre del Mar
Parque Acuático Aquavelis
This is another fun water park that the children will enjoy.
✉ **Urb El Tomillar** ☎ **952 54 27 58** 🕐 **Daily 10–6** 🚌 **Bus from Málaga (Torre del Mar stop)** ♿ **Few** 👍 **Moderate**

Torremolinos
Aquapark
Aquatic attractions here include giant water chutes, water mountains and artificial waves bearing names such as Kamikaze, Cresta Run and Waikiki Surf. The Aquapark also boasts a mini park, restaurant and boutique.
✉ **Ctra de Circunvalación (near Palacio de Congresos)** ☎ **952 38 88 88** 🕐 **May–Sep daily 10–6** 🍴 **Restaurant (££)** ♿ **Few** 👍 **Expensive**

Take Care
When taking children down to southern Spain do remember to take sensible precautions against too much exposure to the sun. It can be exceedingly hot during the summer months, so that protective hats and effective sun lotions are highly advisable.

Costa del Sol & Beyond Attractions

Nightlife

The Costa is famed for its lively night scene, with an abundance of discotheques and nightclubs to suit every taste. There is a concentration of discos in Torremolinos, with a wide choice of glitz to be found in and around the Marbella area, especially Puerto Banús. In Fuengirola and Los Boliches you can find many bars with music, and perhaps a sing-song, a number of which are English-run.

Opening times are flexible; however, the action starts late, very late, with minimal activity to be expected before 11PM or midnight. Once things hot up they seem to carry on well into the early hours. Charges are variable, with some discos charging a fairly substantial entrance fee, which usually includes one free drink.

Casinos

Benalmádena Costa
Casino Torrequebrada
American and French roulette, Black Jack, Punto Blanco, slot machines and private gaming room. Dress is formal and passports must be shown. Piano bar and floor show.

✉ **N340 between Benalmádena Costa and Carvajal** ☎ **952 44 25 45**
🕐 **Daily 8PM–4AM** 🚌 **Bus stop Benalmádena Costa**
💵 **Expensive**

Nueva Andalucía
Casino Marbella
American and French roulette, Black Jack, Stud Caribbean poker, Punto Blanco, slot machines. Jacket and tie required for men. Passport required.

✉ **Hotel Andalucía Plaza, opposite Puerto Banus, Nueva Andalucía** ☎ **952 81 40 00**
🕐 **Daily 9PM–3AM** 🚌 **Bus stop Andalucía Plaza**
💵 **Expensive**

Cinema and Theatre

Among the various cinemas and theatres along the coast, which can be enjoyed by locals and visitors alike, one place stands out as a rock of entertainment for the English-speaking community in the area. The Salon Varietés, which first opened in Fuengirola in 1985, continues to put on a variety of entertainment each season, which is from the middle of September to mid-June. Audiences can enjoy all types of plays, from thrillers to comedies, musicals and pantomines, concerts, flamenco shows and dance festivals, and lectures.

Fuengirola
Cine Sohail
✉ **Avenida Condes de San Isidro s/n** ☎ **952 47 46 41**

Salon Variétés
Cinema and theatre with regular plays and entertainment for the English-speaking community.
✉ **Emancipacón 30** ☎ **952 47 45 42**

Málaga
Alameda Multicines
✉ **Córdoba 13**
☎ **952 21 34 12**

Albéñiz Multicines
✉ **Alcazabilla 4** ☎ **952 21 58 98**

América Multicines
✉ **Explanada de la Estación**
☎ **952 33 99 91**

Andalucía Cinema
✉ **Victoria 2** ☎ **952 21 06 16**

Astoria Cinema
✉ **Plaza de Maria Guerrero**
☎ **952 21 20 64**

Echegaray Cinema
✉ **Echegaray 13** ☎ **952 21 39 99**

Sala Cánovas
Theatre, opera and concerts are performed here in winter with the Málaga Symphony Orchestra.
✉ **Plaza El Ejido** ☎ **952 43 50 07**

Teatro Miguel de Cervantes
Major cultural centre of Málaga with year round

programmes of theatre, opera and concerts.

✉ **Ramos Marín s/n** ☎ **952 22 41 00**

Puerto Banús
Cine Gran Marbella
You can often see films in English at this multi cinema complex.

✉ **Puerto Banús** ☎ **952 81 00 77**

Sevilla
Teatro Municipal Alameda
Varied programme of plays.

✉ **Calle Crédito, s/n** ☎ **954 90 01 62**

Teatro Lope de Vega
Classical concerts are held here.

✉ **Avenida María Luisa s/n** ☎ **954 59 08 53**

Discos
Fuengirola
Discoteca Superstar

✉ **Calle Jacinto Benavente s/n** ☎ **952 47 04 92**

Málaga
Discoteca Bounty

✉ **Plaza Sancha** ☎ **952 22 75 83**

Discoteca Duna

✉ **Avenida J S Elcano 5** ☎ **952 29 08 58**

Discoteca Piano Club Georges

✉ **Mar 90** ☎ **952 22 82 39**

Discoteca Surf

✉ **Calle S Nicolás 2** ☎ **952 22 74 83**

Marbella
Disco Willy Salsa
Another well known disco, popular with the younger set.

✉ **Ctra Cádiz, km 178**

☎ **952 82 73 63**

Mic-Mac Disco-Bar
✉ **Urb Costa Bella 301**
☎ **952 83 39 36**

Olivia Valere
One of the Costa del Sol's favourites. Passport required.

✉ **Hotel Puente Romano, km 184** on the N340 ☎ **952 77 01 00**

Torremolinos
Barbacoa Piano Club

✉ **Urb La Colina s/n** ☎ **952 38 97 49**

Discoteca Caprice

✉ **Paseo Marítimo s/n**
☎ **952 38 18 38**

Gatsby

✉ **Avenida Montemar 36**
☎ **952 38 53 72**

Flamenco and Jazz

Benalmádena Costa
Fortuna Nightclub
International show, flamenco and dancing to live bands.

✉ **Casino Torrequebrada, N340 between Benalmádena Costa and Carvaja** ☎ **952 44 25 45**
🕐 **From 9:30PM**

Mississippi Willow
Lots of entertainment, including concerts, flamenco, the Willow Dixieland Jazz Band and dancing aboard this New Orleans steamboat floating nightclub.

✉ **Puerto Deportivo** ☎ **952 56 01 82**

Córdoba
Mesón Flamenco La Bulería
An old favourite for flamenco.

✉ **Pedro López 3** ☎ **957 48 38 39** 🕐 **Starts at 10:30PM, closed in summer**

Flamenco
Flamenco is closely associated with Andalucía, where its roots belong. For the visitor who wishes to get the flavour of something seen as 'typically Spanish' there are plenty of nightspots along the Costa with flamenco shows which can be colourful and entertaining. The real magic of flamenco, however, is spontaneity and the right ambience, which is not so easy to find. You could experience some good flamenco at a local fiesta, or tucked away in the back streets of towns such as Sevilla or Málaga accompanied, ideally, by someone who knows where to look.

Jazz

Jazz fans have plenty of opportunities to indulge their interest as numerous cafés and piano bars in the main resorts, in particular Torremolinos, Fuengirola, Marbella and Puerto Banús, offer live music which can include jazz, blues and soul. Concerts are also laid on for visiting musicians. These take place in a variety of venues, such as clubs or some of the more prominent hotels along the coast.

The Mississippi-style paddleboat *Willow*, moored in the bay of Puerto Marina Benalmádena, holds jazz concerts by international artists, in addition to regular performances of their own 'resident' Willow Dixieland Band. Enthusiasts can check with local newspapers for a programme of events.

Granada

Jardines Neptuno
Popular but high quality flamenco shows.
✉ **Calle Arabia** ☎ **958 425 11 12** 🕐 **Daily from 10PM**

Málaga

Gloria Bendita
Nightclub with live flamenco shows.
✉ **Avenida Cánovas del Castillo, La Malagueta** ☎ **952 22 72 79**

Teatro Cervantes
The flamenco shows here always attract an enthusiastic audence.
✉ **Ramos Marín** ☎ **952 22 41 00**

Vista Andalucía
✉ **Avenida de los Guindos s/n** ☎ **952 23 11 57** 🕐 **Tue–Sun 10:30PM–6AM, closed Mon**

Marbella

La Caseta del Casino
Shows of flamenco dancing and *sevillanas*.
✉ **Casino Nueva Andalucía, Andalucía Plaza Hotel, N340, Nueva Andalucía.** ☎ **952 81 40 00** 🕐 **From midnight in summer**

Nerja

El Colonio
Restaurant with performances of flamenco in attractive Andalucían house.
✉ **Granada 6** ☎ **952 52 18 26** 🕐 **Dinner show at 9:30 or 10PM Wed–Fri in summer. 9PM Wed in winter**

Sevilla

Los Gallos
Small and intimate, considered to be among the top shows.
✉ **Plaza de Santa Cruz** ☎ **954 21 69 81** 🕐 **Shows at 9 and 11PM**

Torremolinos

El Vito de Trini
Regular flamenco shows.
✉ **Centro Comercial Duquesa de España 342, km 222,9** ☎ **952 37 23 70**

Molino de la Bóveda
Flamenco and South American guitar music.
✉ **Cuesta del Tajo 8** ☎ **952 38 11 85**

Taberna Flamenco Pepe López
Well known for flamenco and folk dancing.
✉ **Plaza de la Gamba Alegre** ☎ **952 38 12 84** 🕐 **Daily at 10PM Apr to autumn.**

Sport

Along the Costa del Sol bullfights are held on Sunday afternoons during the summer season in Málaga, Estepona and Marbella. The bigger names, however, are attracted by Sevilla, Córdoba and other prominent towns in Andalucía.

Other spectator sports include soccer, basketball, tennis and golf, such as the World Cup, the Spanish and the Ryder cups. Polo matches are held in Sotogrande from July to September. Check with local publications for details of matches and events.

In the Air

Aeroclub
Can arrange for para-sailing and hang-gliding.
✉ **Ctra de Cádiz, Málaga** ☎ **952 23 05 95**

Aviación del Sol
Organises hot air balloon trips over land and sea.

☒ **Marbella** ☎ 952 87 72 49
and ☒ **Apartado de Correos
344, Ronda** ☎ 952 87 72 49

Escuela Parapente el Valle
☒ **Valle de Abdalajís, Málaga**
☎ 952 48 91 80

Free-Flying School
Organises hang-gliding and
delta-winging courses
☒ **Granada**

Gliding Centre
☒ **Area de Deportes,
Ayuntamiento de Antequera**
☎ 952 84 42 11

Delta-winging in Abdalajís
Valley and at Los Cerros de
Mijas.

Golf

The majority of golf clubs
require a handicap certificate.
Courses get booked up by
members so visitors are
advised to book well in
advance to ensure a game.
Green fees vary according to
season. (A rough guide to
green fees is given in the
panel on the right.) There are
numerous competitions open
to visitors throughout the
year. Useful publications
include:
Golf in Andalucia ☒ **Calle
Calvario 8, Marbella** ☎ 952 82
89 76, and *Revista Costa Golf*
☒ **Apartado Correos 358,
Torremolinos. The Federación
Andaluza de Golf** ☒ **Calle
Sierra de Grazalema 33, bloque
5, 29016 Málaga** ☎ 952 22 55
99/90 is a useful source of
information

Benahavis
Monte Mayor Golf Club (££)
18 holes, par 70.
☒ **Urb. Los Naranjos Country
Club** ☎ 952 11 30 88

Benalmádena
Golf Torrequebrada (££)
18 holes, par 72.
☒ **Ctra de Cádiz, N340** ☎ 952
44 27 42

Estepona
**Atalaya Golf and Country
Club (££)**
27 holes, par 72; golf school
offers week-long and
weekend courses.
☒ **Ctra Benahavis km 0.7**
☎ 952 88 28 12

**Club de Golf Coto La
Sorena (£)**
9 holes, par 3.
☒ **Ctra N340 163.5** ☎ 952 80
47 00

Estepona Golf (£)
18 holes, par 72.
☒ **Apartado 532**
☎ 952 11 30 81

Golf el Paraíso (£)
18 holes, par 71.
☒ **Ctra N340** ☎ 952 88 38 46

Málaga
**Alhaurin Golf & Country
Club (£)**
45 holes, par 72.
☒ **Mijas–Alhaurin el Grand,
km6** ☎ 952 59 59 70

**Guadalhorce Club de Golf
(£)**
18 holes, par 72.
☒ **Ctra de Cádiz (Churriana
crossroads)** ☎ 952 24 36 82

Manilva
La Duquesa (£)
18 holes, par 72.
☎ 952 89 04 25

Marbella
Aloha Golf Club (£££)
27 holes, par 72.
☒ **Nueva Andalucia** ☎ 952
81 37 50

Golf
Green fees:
£   = Ptas 2,750–6,050
££   = Ptas 6,050–9,350
£££ = Ptas 9,350–22,000

Costa del Golf

Golf has had a tremendous impact on the Costa del Sol area, especially during the winter season. Its mild winter climate, combined with an abundance of high quality courses, make it a highly desirable year-round golfing destination, sometimes described as the Costa del Golf.

Spain's hosting of the Ryder Cup in 1997 brought great presige to the area, earning it international acclaim. It was a matter of great pride to the Costa that the Valderrama Golf Course in Sotogrande was the first course selected outside the UK and US to host this great international event.

In November of 1999 the Valderrama Golf Course was again in the golfing spotlight as the venue for the American Express Championship '99, part of the new World Golf Championship Tournament.

Club de Golf Las Brisas (£££)
18 holes, par 72.
✉ Nueva Andalucía ☎ 952 81 08 75

La Dame de Noche (£)
9 holes, par 70.
✉ Ctra N340, km192 ☎ 952 81 81 50

Golf Club Marbella (£££)
18 holes, par 71.
✉ Ctra de Cádiz, km188
☎ 952 83 05 00

Golf Río Real (££)
18 holes, par 72.
✉ Ctra N340 ☎ 952 77 95 09

Guadalmina Club de Golf (££)
36 holes, par 71.
✉ San Pedro de Alcántara
☎ 952 88 33 75

La Quinta Golf & Country Club (££)
27 holes, par 72. School with training programme designed by Manuel Piñero (☎ 952 76 23 03).
✉ Nueva Andalucía ☎ 952 76 23 90

Santo Maria Golf (££)
9 holes, par 70.
✉ Ctra N340 ☎ 952 83 03 88

Mijas

Campo de Golf Miraflores (£)
18 holes, par 70.
✉ Urb. Riviera Golf, Mijas-Costa ☎ 952 93 16 90

Club de Golf La Siesta (£)
✉ Urb Sitio de Calahonda, Mijas-Costa ☎ 952 83 63 70

Urb Mijas Golf (££)
36 holes, par 72.
✉ 3km from Fuengirola (old road to Coín) ☎ 952 47 68 43

San Roque/ Sotogrande

La Alcaidesa (££)
18 holes, par 72.
✉ Apartado 125, San Roque
☎ 956 79 10 40

Club de Golf Sotogrande (£££)
27 holes, par 72.
✉ Urb Sotogrande, Cádiz
☎ 955 79 50 50

Club de Golf Valderrama (£££)
18 holes, par 72.
✉ Urb Sotogrande, Cádiz
☎ 956 79 57 75

San Roque Club (££)
18 holes, par 72.
✉ San Roque ☎ 956 61 30 30

Horseriding

Estepona

Finca Siesta
Picnic and beach rides; lessons in dressage and showjumping.
✉ Km 163 on N230 (opposite Hacienda Beach) ☎ 952 79 01 89

Marbella

Club Hípico Elviria
✉ Zona Las Chapas, El Platero
☎ 952 77 06 75

Los Monteros Hotel
Lessons and rides into surrounding hills.
✉ N340, 2km east of Marbella
☎ 952 77 06 75

San Pedro de Alcántara

Lakeview Equestrian Centre
Qualified instruction in dressage and showjumping; private or group lessons.
✉ Valle del Sol ☎ 952 78 69 34

San Roque
The San Roque Club Equestrian Centre
For beginners and experienced riders. One hour or full day hacks. Private or group tuition (2,500 ptas per hour).
✉ San Roque Club Suites Hotel, Ctra Cádiz km 126.5 ☎ 956 61 32 32

Sotogrande Polo
You can experience the thrill of riding top class polo ponies on Sotogrande's polo fields. One hour lessons cost 7,000 ptas.
☎ 956 79 64 64

Torre del Mar
Lavao Villalba
✉ J Ctra V Alméria s/n ☎ 952 54 14 43

Torremolinos
Hípica International
Lessons in dressage and jumping. One hour hacks for experienced riders (2,000 ptas). Refreshments available.
✉ Camino de la Sierra ☎ 952 43 55 49

González-Garrido
✉ J Ctra de Cádiz s/n ☎ 952 38 30 63

El Ranchito
✉ Camino del Pilar, La Colina (Torremolinos) ☎ 952 38 30 63

Lawn Bowls

Fuengirola
First Lawn Bowls Club
First bowls club to have been opened in Spain, with 7-rink grass green.
✉ Las Palmeras Complex, near the beach ☎ 952 47 10 63
🕐 Club days are Tue, Thu and Sat

Marbella
Santa Maria Bowls
The club has two greens with facilities for hiring bowls and coaching from the Spanish National champion. There is also a bar and a restaurant.
✉ Coto Los Dolones, CN-340 km 192 ☎ 952 83 84 19
🕐 Open 7 days a week. Club afternoons Tue and Thur

Superbowl
Club meetings are organised by champion bowling owners, with the clubhouse open to all visitors.
✉ Nueva Andalucía ☎ 952 81 77 13

San Pedro de Alcántara
Bena Vista Bowling Club
Visitors are welcome at Bena Vista Bowling Club and tuition is available for beginners. Clubhouse and bar on the premises.
✉ El Paraíso complex, 4km west of San Pedro ☎ 952 88 82 44

Tennis

Benalmádena Costa
Club de Tenis Torrequebrada
✉ Urb Torrequebrada, Ctra de Cádiz ☎ 952 44 10 07

Estepona
Club de Tennis Estepona
10 courts, 3 floodlit; cement and tennis-quick.
✉ Urb Forest Hill ☎ 952 80 15 79

Hotel Atalaya Park
9 floodlit courts, tennis-quick.
✉ Ctra de Cádiz, km168.5 ☎ 952 78 13 00

Polo
Another string to Sotogrande's bow is the sport of polo, which continues to thrive.
Top ranking players come here to take part in the numerous matches which are held regularly during the summer months at the Santa María Polo Club. The sport has a substantial following, attracting an enthusiastic crowd. Although a traditional sport, with continuity within families, efforts are being made to popularise the sport and to bring it within reach of a wider public.

Clean Beaches

In the mid 1980s a decree was passed in Andalucía establishing the standards to be maintained with regard to the cleanliness of its beaches. The matter is taken very seriously and carefully monitored by the authorities, with the result that an ever increasing number of beaches can be seen proudly displaying the coveted Blue Flag. Beaches are classified by 5 to 1 stars according to their condition. Symbols also indicate the 'dos and don'ts', while other signs advertise services available on the beach. Visitors are requested to observe these golden rules: be sure to use a protective sun block, especially where children are concerned; drink plenty of liquid (but do check if the water is safe to drink); make sure any food consumed has been bought in a reputable place; keep the beaches clean by using containers for rubbish disposal; use a mat or towel when relaxing on the sand; do not swim in prohibited areas; respect the 'dangerous to swim' sign; do not take pets onto the beach; camp only in authorised areas which have proper facilities.

Fuengirola

Club Doña Sofía
✉ P Doña Sofía ☎ 952 47 50 84

Málaga

Club El Candado
7 floodlit courts, cement and tennis-quick.
✉ Urb El Candado ☎ 952 29 08 45

Club de Tenis Andaluz
3 courts, tennis-quick.
✉ Ctra de Málaga–Almería, km 297.8 ☎ 952 52 09 48

Club de Tenis Málaga
11 courts, 8 floodlit; clay and tennis-quick.
✉ Urb San Antón ☎ 952 29 10 92

Laguna Beach
8 floodlit courts, cement.
✉ Urb Laguna Beach, Torrox ☎ 952 53 00 00

Marbella

Centro de Tenis Don Carlos
11 courts, 4 floodlit; clay and tennis-quick.
✉ Urb Elviria, Ctra de Cádiz ☎ 952 83 17 39

Club Manolo Santana
✉ Hotel Puente Romano Ctra de Cádiz ☎ 952 82 61 03

Club Hotel Los Monteros
10 courts, 2 floodlit, tennis-quick.
✉ Ctra de Cádiz, km194 ☎ 952 77 17 00

Mijas

Club del Sol
12 courts, 5 floodlit.
✉ Sitio de Calahonde. Mijas-Costa ☎ 952 83 08 30

Lew Hoad Campo de Tenis
8 courts, tennis-quick. Clinics and courses are held here.

✉ Ctra de Mijas ☎ 952 47 48 58

Tennis Centre Aquarius
7 courts, 4 floodlit, tennis-quick.
✉ Urb Riviera del Sol, Mijas-Costa ☎ 952 83 39 40

Torremolinos

Club Hotel Don Pablo
7 floodlit courts, tennis-quick.
✉ Paseo Marítimo ☎ 952 38 38 88

Club de Tenis Torremolinos
5 courts, 3 floodlit, tennis-quick.
✉ Cañada de Churriana ☎ 952 43 51 25

Watersports

Sailing

There are good facilities at all the major marinas. Yachts for charter with crew from:

R&N
✉ Marbella ☎ 952 65 89 39

Victoria A
✉ Marbella ☎ 952 45 67 50

Sailing Courses:

Club de Mar de Puerto Banús
Prices for tuition start from around Ptas 2,000 per hour for beginners; rentals range from Ptas 1,500–8,000 per hour. Also windsurfing.

Scuba Diving

Courses for scuba diving are held at the Scuba Diving School in Puerto Marina, Benalmádena. Otherwise, one of the best spots for this sport is around Nerja.

Club Nautique
Day courses with fully

qualified instructors; up to 12m dives.

✉ **Marina del Este, near Almuñecar** ☎ **958 82 75 14**

Club Nautico Diving Centre
Year-round courses, equipment hire included. Daily trips from the marina.

✉ **Puerto Marina de Benalmádena** ☎ **952 56 07 69**

Swimming
The beaches of the Costa del Sol vary from sand to fine grit and shingle. Some of the best sandy beaches are around Torremolinos, Fuengirola and on either side of Marbella, all of which can become very crowded in the summer season. For more secluded beaches try the coast east of Málaga or west of Estepona.

Waterskiing and Windsurfing
There are plenty of opportunities for water skiing and windsurfing along the western Costa del Sol. Facilities and tuition are available in all major resorts, often from the hotels. Top spot for windsurfing is at Tarifa, where strong winds provide favourable conditions.

BIC Sports Centre
Daily lessons for beginners and more advanced; one-week package available.

✉ **Hotel dos Mares, Ctra Cádiz km79.5, Tarifa** ☎ **956 68 40 35**

Club El Oceano
Waterskiing, dinghy and boardsailing.

✉ **Torrenueva Playa, Mijas-Costa** ☎ **952 49 33 25**

Club Mistral
Wind boards for rent on the beach Ptas 2–4,000 for three hours; lessons from Ptas 16,000 per hour.

✉ **Tarifa** ☎ **952 68 43 26**

Hotel Balcón de España
✉ **Ctra N340, km76, Tarifa**
☎ **952 68 43**

Hotel Hurricane
✉ **Ctra N340, km77** ☎ **952 68 49 19**

Winter Sports
From November until May it is possible to enjoy winter sports in the Sierra Nevada, to the south of Granada, not far from the coast.

Sol y Nieve (Sun and Snow)
This ski resort offers good facilities, with ski-lifts and chair-lifts, a tourist complex and all kinds of skiing.

✉ **35km from Granada, and some 100km from the coast**
🕒 **Dec–Apr**

Sierra Nevada Club
The World Alpine Ski Championships are now hosted annually in the Sierra Granada and the Sierra Nevada, establishing the area as a force in the international world of skiing.

☎ **958 24 91 11**

For information on the Bonal bus service between Granada and the Sierra Nevada ☎ 958 27 31 00/27 24 97; for taxis ☎ 958 15 14 61 or 28 06 54; for information regarding road conditions ☎ 958 28 24 00 or 28 24 50; to listen to a recorded message about the skiing conditions ☎ 958 24 91 19.

Sierra Nevada
The Sierra Nevada is the most southerly ski resort in Europe and one of the highest, which gives it a long season (sometimes lasting well into May). Its proximity to the coast gives the possibility of swimming in the sea and skiing on snowy slopes on the same day!

The resort is easily accessible by car from Málaga (161km) and from Granada (35km) which also operates a daily bus service to the centre.

What's On When

Festivals

Year round, Spaniards delight in their *ferias* and *fiestas*. With their colour and exuberance they are celebrations of life itself. Many are religious events, such as Holy Week and Corpus Christi. There are pilgrimages, celebrations for patron saints, lively fairs and festivals connected with fishermen and the sea. Flamenco fairs and bullfight festivals, concerts and numerous cultural events add to the list.

Verdiales

Worth seeing, if possible, is a performance of the *Verdiales*, who are unique to the province of Málaga. These musicians form groups known as *pandas*, and are led by an *alcalde* (mayor) with a beribboned baton. Their outfits, music and dancing are most unusual and involve much flag waving. They participate in various celebrations in addition to the main festival of the *Verdiales* held in late December.

January

Los Reyes Magos (6 January, Málaga). The Three Kings throw sweets to children from grand floats.

February/March

Carnaval (the week before Lent). In Málaga, Granada and Antequera. An exuberant affair with floats, colourful costumes, music and dancing.

March

Semana Santa (Holy Week, moveable date). In Sevilla, Málaga and Granada. From Palm Sunday to Easter Day there are nightly processions of *cofradías* (brotherhoods) carrying images of the saints or the Virgin; wearing pointed hoods, each carries a lighted candle. The muffled drums are accompanied by the occasional *saeta* (an improvised religious lament).

April

Fería de Sevilla (Seville Fair). Originally a cattle fair, the Fair has evolved into a world famous event of colour, music and dancing. The daily horseback parade is a special attraction with the men in dashing outfits, and their ladies decked out in traditional flamboyant dresses. Every afternoon bullfights take place in the Maestranza ring with the most famous of Spain's matadors.

May

Las Cruces de Mayo (early May). This represents an ancient custom when crosses decorated with both real and paper flowers are placed in the streets and squares. The fiesta is particularly attractive in Torrox and Coín.

May/June

Corpus Christi (moveable date). Processions along flower strewn streets. Especially colourful in Granada, with parades, music and dancing.

July

La Virgen del Carmen (16 July). Most spectacualr at Los Boliches, Fuengirola; also at Estepona, Marbella and Nerja. The patron saint of fishermen is paraded through the streets before being taken around the bay on a boat; fireworks, music and dancing on the beach.

September

Pedro Romero Fiestas (early Sep). Ronda celebrates the bullfighter with *corridas Goyescas* (Goya-style bullfights) with performances by top matadors in the costume of Goya's time.

October

Feria del Rosario. This fair is celebrated in Fuengirola during the first two weeks in October. *Casetas* (club-houses) of various societies and brotherhoods set up between Fuengirola and Los Boliches offer shows, food and drink. A lively affair, with horse-riding events, flamenco and fireworks.

December

Fiesta de Verdiales (28 December). In the Venta del Túnel, just north of Málaga. Colourfully attired *pandas* (musical groups) compete with each other; a very lively event with music, food and wine.

Practical
Matters

Before You Go   118
When You Are There   119–23
Language   124

TIME DIFFERENCES

GMT 12 noon	Spain 1PM →	Germany 1PM →	USA (NY) 7AM ←	Netherlands 1PM →

BEFORE YOU GO

WHAT YOU NEED

● Required ○ Suggested ▲ Not required	UK	Germany	USA	Netherlands
Passport/National Identity Card	●	●	●	●
Visa	▲	▲	▲	▲
Onward or Return Ticket	▲	▲	▲	▲
Health Inoculations	▲	▲	●	▲
Health Documentation (reciprocal agreement document) (➤ 123, Health)	●	●	▲	●
Travel Insurance	○	○	○	○
Driving Licence (national – EU format/national/Spanish trnsltn/interntnl)	●	●	●	●
Car Insurance Certificate (if own car)	●	●	●	●
Car Registration Document (if own car)	●	●	●	●

WHEN TO GO

Average figures for Costa del Sol

High season

Low season

16°C	17°C	18°C	21°C	23°C	27°C	29°C	29°C	27°C	23°C	19°C	17°C
JAN	FEB	MAR	APR	MAY	JUN	JUL	AUG	SEP	OCT	NOV	DEC

Wet   Cloud   Sun   Sunshine & showers

TOURIST OFFICES

In the UK
Spanish Tourist Office,
22/23 Manchester Square,
London W1M 5AP
☎ (0171) 486 8077
Fax: (0171) 486 8034

In the USA
Tourist Office of Spain,
666 Fifth Avenue 35th,
New York, NY 10103
☎ (212) 265 8822
Fax: (212) 265 8864

Tourist Office of Spain,
8383 Wilshire Boulevard,
Suite 960,
Beverley Hills, Cal 90211
☎ (213) 658 7192
Fax: (213) 658 1061

POLICE (Policía Nacional) 091; (Policía Local) 092

AMBULANCE (Ambulancia) 061

FIRE (Bomberos) 080 or 230 60 60 (Málaga); 277 43 49

(Marbella); 238 39 39 (Torremolinos)

WHEN YOU ARE THERE

ARRIVING

Most visitors to the Costa del Sol arrive at Málaga Airport (☎ 952 04 88 04). Spain's national airline, Iberia (☎ 302 40 05 00), operates direct scheduled flights to Málaga from major European and North American cities. The other nearest airport is Seville.

Málaga Airport
Kilometres to city centre

10 kilometres

Journey times	
🚆	12 minutes
🚌	20 minutes
🚗	20 minutes

Seville Airport
Kilometres to city centre

8 kilometres

Journey times	
🚆	N/A
🚌	20 minutes
🚗	20 minutes

MONEY

Spain's currency is the peseta, issued in notes of 1,000, 2,000, 5,000 and 10,000 pesetas and coins of 5, 10, 25, 50, 100, 200 and 500 pesetas. A one-peseta coin still exists. Travellers' cheques are accepted by most hotels, shops and restaurants in lieu of cash. Travellers' cheques in pesetas are the most convenient. The euro will start circulation on 1 January 2002, with the peseta due to be phased out on 1 July 2002.

TIME

 Spain is one hour ahead of Greenwich Mean Time (GMT+1), but from late March until the last Sunday in September, summer time (GMT+2) operates.

CUSTOMS

 CUSTOMS ALLOWANCES

Goods Bought Outside the EU (Duty-Free Limits):
Alcohol: 1 litre of spirits over 22% volume, OR 2 litres of fortified wine, sparkling wine or other liqueurs, PLUS 2 litres of still table wine
Tobacco: 200 cigarettes, OR 100 cigarillos, OR 50 cigars, OR 250g of tobacco
Perfume: 50ml
Toilet water: 250ml
Gifts: up to 6,200 ptas per adult and 3,200 ptas per child

Goods Bought Inside the EU for Your Own Use (Limits):
Alcohol: 1.5 litres of spirits, OR 3 litres of fortified wine, sparkling wine or other liqueurs, PLUS 5 litres of wine
Tobacco: 300 cigarettes, OR 150 cigarillos, OR 75 cigars, OR 400g of tobacco

(For tobacco and alcohol allowances visitors must be 17 and over)

 NO

Drugs, firearms, ammunition, offensive weapons, obscene material, unlicensed animals.

119

UK
952 21 75 71
(Málaga)

Germany
952 21 24 42
(Málaga)

USA
952 47 48 91
(Fuengirola)

Netherlands
952 27 99 54
(Málaga)

WHEN YOU ARE THERE

TOURIST OFFICES

Costa del Sol
● Costa del Sol Tourist Board
Palacio de Congresos
Calle México s/n
29620 Torremolinos
☎ 952 05 86 94/95
Fax: 952 05 03 11

Towns/Resorts
● Plaza San Sebastian 7,
Antequera
☎ 952 70 25 05

● Carretera de Cádiz, Km 220,
Benalmádena Costa
☎ 952 35 00 61

● Avenida San Lorenzo,
Estepona
☎ 952 80 20 02

● Avenida Jesús Santos
Rein 6, Fuengirola
☎ 952 46 76 25

● Plaza Mariana Pineda 12,
Granada
☎ 958 22 66 88

● Pasaje de Chinitas 4,
Málaga
☎ 952 21 34 45

● Glorieta de la Fontanilla,
Marbella
☎ 952 77 14 42

● Calle Puerta del Mar 2,
Nerja
☎ 952 52 15 31

● Avenida de Andalucía 119,
Torre del Mar
☎ 952 54 11 04

● Plaza de las Comunidades
Autónomas, s/n (Bajondillo
Beach) Torremolinos
☎ 952 37 19 09

NATIONAL HOLIDAYS

J	F	M	A	M	J	J	A	S	O	N	D
2	1	1	1	1	1	1	1		1	1	3

1 Jan	New Year's Day
6 Jan	Epiphany
28 Feb	Andalucian Day (regional)
Mar/Apr	Maundy Thursday, Good Friday, Easter Monday
1 May	Labour Day
24 Jun	San Juan (regional)
25 Jul	Santiago (regional)
15 Aug	Assumption of the Virgin
12 Oct	National Day
1 Nov	All Saints' Day
6 Dec	Constitution Day
8 Dec	Feast of the Immaculate Conception
25 Dec	Christmas Day

OPENING HOURS

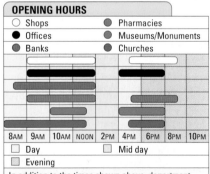

○ Shops ● Pharmacies
● Offices ● Museums/Monuments
● Banks ● Churches

| 8AM | 9AM | 10AM | NOON | 2PM | 4PM | 6PM | 8PM | 10PM |

☐ Day ☐ Mid day
☐ Evening

In addition to the times shown above, department stores, large supermarkets and shops in tourist resorts open from 10AM through to 8, 9 or even 10PM. The vast majority of shops close Sun and some close in Aug. Some banks open Sat (Oct–May only) 8:30AM to 1PM. The opening times of museums is just a rough guide; some open longer in summer, while hours may be reduced in winter. Many museums close Sun afternoon, some also on Sat afternoon, as well as Mon or another day in the week. Some museums offer free entry to EU citizens (take your passport). **Remember – all opening times are subject to change.**

DRIVE ON THE
RIGHT

TOILETS
CHARGE

PUBLIC TRANSPORT

 Internal Flights The national airline, Iberia, plus the smaller Aviaco, operate an extensive network of internal flights. The main office of Iberia is at Calle Molina Lario 13, Málaga (☎ 952 13 61 47). For reservations on domestic flights (☎ 902 40 05 00). Not cheap but worth considering if

 Trains Services are provided by the state-run company – RENFE. Fares are among the cheapest in Europe. A useful service is the coastal route from Málaga to Fuengirola, via Torremolinas and Benalmádena, with a stop at the airport. Trains run every 30 minutes between 6AM and 11PM (☎ RENFE Malaga 952 12 82 63 or 952 36 02 02).

 Buses There is a comprehensive and reliable bus network operated by different companies along the coast and to inland towns and villages. Fares are very reasonable. Go to the local bus station for details of routes. The bus station in Málaga (☎ 952 35 00 61) is just behind the RENFE train station.

 Ferries A service runs from Málaga to Melilla (Morocco), run by Trasmediterránea (☎ 952 22 43 91), taking 10 hours. A shorter route to Morocco is from Algeciras to Ceuta (1½ hours) and Tangier – via Gibraltar – (2½ hours) run by ISNASA (☎ 956 65 37 06), Trasmediterránea (☎ 956 66 52 00), and Transtour (☎ 956 65 37 06).

 Urban Transport Traffic in the main towns and resorts of the Costa del Sol is normally heavy, especially in summer, but public transport in the form of buses is generally good. If arriving in Málaga by train, bus No 3 runs from the RENFE station to the city centre every 10 minutes.

CAR RENTAL

 The leading international car rental companies operate on the Costa del Sol and you can hire a car in advance (essential at peak periods) either direct or through a travel agent. Airlines may offer 'fly-drive' deals. Hiring from a local firm, though, is usually cheaper.

TAXIS

 Only use taxis which display a licence issued by the local authority. Taxis show a green light when available for hire. They can be flagged down in the street. In cities and large towns taxis are metered; where they are not, determine the price of the journey in advance.

DRIVING

 Speed limits on *autopistas* (toll motorways) and *autovías* (free motorways): **120kph**; dual carriageways and roads with overtaking lanes: **100kph**. Take care on the N340 coastal highway. Cars travel at tremendous speed and this road is labelled as a dangerous one.

 Speed limits on country roads: **90kph**

 Speed limits on urban roads: **50kph**; in residential areas:

 Must be worn in front seats at all times and in rear seats where fitted.

 Random breath-testing. Limit: 0.8gm alcohol per 1,000cm³ breath.

 Fuel (*gasolina*) is available in four grades: *Normal* (92 octane); *Super* (98 octane); *Sin plomo* (unleaded, 95 and 98 octane); and *gasoleo* or *gasoil* (diesel). Petrol prices are fixed by the Government and are similar to those in the

 If you break down with your own car and are a member of an AIT-affiliated motoring club, call the Real Automóvil Club de España, or RACE (☎ 915 93 33 33) for assistance. If the car is hired you should follow the instructions in the documentation; most international rental firms provide a rescue service.

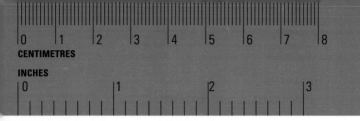

PERSONAL SAFETY

Snatching of handbags and cameras, pick-pocketing, theft of unattended baggage and car break-ins are the principal crimes against visitors. Any crime or loss should be reported to the national police force (Policía Nacional) who wear brown uniforms. Some precautions:

- Do not leave valuables on the beach or poolside
- Place valuables in a hotel safety-deposit box
- Wear handbags and cameras across your chest
- Avoid lonely, seedy and dark areas at night

Police assistance:
☎ **091**
from any call box

TELEPHONES

All telephone numbers throughout Spain now consist of nine digits (incorporating the former area code, preceded by 9), and no matter where you call from you must always dial all nine digits. A public telephone (*teléfono*) takes 25-, 100- and 500-peseta coins. A phonecard (*credifone*) is available from post offices and some shops for 1,000 or 2,000 pesetas.

International Dialling Codes

From Spain to:

UK:	**00 44**
Germany:	**00 49**
USA:	**00 1**
Netherlands:	**00 31**

POST

Post Offices
Post offices (*correos*) are generally open as below; in main centres they may open extended hours. Málaga's main post office is at Avenida de Andalucía 1. Stamps (*sellos*) can also be bought at tobacconists (*estancos*).
Open: 9–2 (1PM Sat)
Closed: Sun
☎ 952 35 90 08 (Málaga)

ELECTRICITY

The power supply is: 220/230 volts (in some bathrooms and older buildings: 110/120 volts).

Type of socket: round two-hole sockets taking round plugs of two round pins.
British visitors will need an adaptor and US visitors a voltage transformer.

TIPS/GRATUITIES

Yes ✓ No ✗		
Restaurants (if service not included)	✓	5–10%
Cafés/bars	✓	change
Taxis	✓	2–3%
Tour guides	✓	change
Porters	✓	change
Chambermaids	✓	change
Hairdressers	✓	change
Cloakroom attendants	✓	change
Theatre/cinema usherettes	✓	change
Toilets	✓	change

PHOTOGRAPHY

What to photograph: the rugged coast, unspoilt inland villages, examples of Moorish architecture, and panoramas of the Sierra Nevada.

Best times to photograph: the summer sun can be too bright at the height of the day making photos taken at this time appear 'flat'. It is best to take photographs in the early morning or late evening.

Where to buy film: film (*rollo/carrete*) and camera batteries (*pilas*) are readily available from tourist shops, department stores and photo shops.

HEALTH

Insurance

Nationals of EU and certain other countries can get free medical treatment in Spain with the relevant documentation (Form E111 for Britons) although private medical insurance is still advised and is essential for all other visitors.

Dental Services

Dental treatment normally has to be paid for in full as dentists operate privately. A list of *dentistas* can be found in the yellow pages of the telephone directory. Dental treatment should be covered by private medical insurance.

Sun Advice

The sunniest (and hottest) months are July and August when daytime temperatures are often into the 30°s C. Try to avoid the midday sun and use a high-factor sun cream to start with, and allow yourself to become used to the sun gradually.

Drugs

Prescriptions and non-prescription drugs and medicines are available from pharmacies (*farmácias*), distinguished by a large green cross. They are able to dispense many drugs which would be available only on prescription in other countries.

Safe Water

Tap water is chlorinated and generally safe to drink; however, unfamiliar water may cause mild abdominal upsets. Mineral water (*agua mineral*) is cheap and widely available. It is sold *sin gas* (still) and *con gas* (carbonated).

CONCESSIONS

Students/Youths Holders of an International Student Identity Card (ISIC) may be able to obtain some concessions on travel, entrance fees etc, but the Costa del Sol is not really geared up for students (special facilities and programmes are limited). The main advantage for students and young people is that low-cost package deals are available.

Senior Citizens The Costa del Sol is an excellent destination for older travellers – travel agents offer tailored package holidays. In the winter months there are special low-cost, long-stay holidays for senior citizens; the best deals are available through tour operators who specialise in holidays for senior citizens.

CLOTHING SIZES

Spain	UK	Rest of Europe	USA	
46	36	46	36	Suits
48	38	48	38	Suits
50	40	50	40	Suits
52	42	52	42	Suits
54	44	54	44	Suits
56	46	56	46	Suits
41	7	41	8	Shoes
42	7.5	42	8.5	Shoes
43	8.5	43	9.5	Shoes
44	9.5	44	10.5	Shoes
45	10.5	45	11.5	Shoes
46	11	46	12	Shoes
37	14.5	37	14.5	Shirts
38	15	38	15	Shirts
39/40	15.5	39/40	15.5	Shirts
41	16	41	16	Shirts
42	16.5	42	16.5	Shirts
43	17	43	17	Shirts
34	8	34	6	Dresses
36	10	36	8	Dresses
38	12	38	10	Dresses
40	14	40	12	Dresses
42	16	42	14	Dresses
44	18	44	16	Dresses
38	4.5	38	6	Shoes
38	5	38	6.5	Shoes
39	5.5	39	7	Shoes
39	6	39	7.5	Shoes
40	6.5	40	8	Shoes
41	7	41	8.5	Shoes

WHEN DEPARTING

- Remember to contact the airport or airline on the day prior to leaving to ensure that the flight details are unchanged.
- There is no airport departure tax to pay so you can happily spend your last remaining pesetas.
- Spanish customs are usually polite and normally easy to negotiate.

LANGUAGE

Spanish is one of the easiest languages. All vowels are pure and short (as in English). Some useful tips on speaking: 'c' is lisped before 'e' and 'i', otherwise hard; 'h' is silent; 'j' is pronounced like a guttural 'j'; 'r' is rolled; 'v' sounds more like 'b'; and 'z' is the same as a soft 'c'. English is widely spoken in the principal resorts but you will get a better reception if you at least try communicating with Spaniards in their own tongue. More extensive coverage can be found in the AA's *Essential Spanish Phrase Book* which lists over 2,000 phrases and 2,000 words.

hotel	*hotel*	breakfast	*desayuno*
room	*habitación*	toilet	*lavabo*
single/double	*individual/doble*	bath	*baño*
one/two nights	*una/dos noche(s)*	shower	*ducha*
per person/per	*por persona/por*	en suite	*en su habitación*
room	*habitación*	balcony	*balcón*
reservation	*reserva*	key	*llave*
rate	*precio*	chambermaid	*camarera*

bank	*banco*	American dollar	*dólar*
exchange office	*oficina de cambio*		*estadounidense*
post office	*correos*	bank card	*tarjeta del banco*
cashier	*cajero*	credit card	*tarjeta de crédito*
money	*dinero*	giro bank card	*tarjeta de la caja*
coin	*moneda*		*postal*
foreign currency	*moneda extranjera*	cheque	*cheque*
change money	*cambiar dinero*	traveller's cheque	*cheque de viajero*
pound sterling	*libra esterlina*	giro cheque	*cheque postal*

restaurant	*restaurante*	snack	*merienda*
bar	*bar*	starter	*primer plato*
table	*mesa*	dish	*plato*
menu	*carta*	main course	*plato principal*
tourist menu	*menú turístico*	dessert	*postre*
wine list	*carta de vinos*	drink	*bebida*
lunch	*almuerzo*	waiter	*camarero*
dinner	*cena*	bill	*cuenta*

aeroplane	*avión*	ferry	*transbordador*
airport	*aeropuerto*	port	*puerto*
flight	*vuelo*	ticket	*billete*
train	*tren*	..single/return	*ida/ida y vuelta*
..station	*estación ferrocarril*	..first/second class	*primera/segunda*
bus	*autobús*		*clase*
..station	*estación de*	timetable	*horario*
	autobúses	seat	*asiento*
..stop	*parada de autobús*	non-smoking	*no fumadores*

yes	*sí*	help!	*ayuda!*
no	*no*	today	*hoy*
please	*por favor*	tomorrow	*mañana*
thank you	*gracias*	yesterday	*ayer*
hello	*hola*	how much?	*cuánto?*
goodbye	*adiós*	expensive	*caro*
good night	*buenas noches*	open	*abierto*
excuse me	*perdóneme*	closed	*cerrado*

INDEX

accommodation 13, 98–101
agriculture 7
La Alcazaba 16
Alcázar de los Reyes Cristianos 52
Los Alcornocales 12
La Alhambra 17, 63
Alhaurín el Grande 49
Almuñecar 42–3
Las Alpujarras 12, 13
Andalucía 12, 79
Antequera 44–5, 88
antique shops 102
aqua parks 106, 107
Arroya de la Miel 47

Balcón de Europa 70
banks 120
Baños Romanos 45
Basílica de Vega del Mar 78
beaches 55, 114
Benalmádena 13, 106
Benalmádena Costa 46, 106
Benalmádena Pueblo 47, 106
Benalmádena Puerto Marina 48
birdwatching 13
Los Boliches 60
Bonsai Museum 67
bookstores 102
Las Bovedas 78
bowls 113
bullfighting 74–5
Bullfighting Museum 53
Burriana 70
buses 121

Calahonda 13, 70
Caleta de Vélez 85
Capilla Real, Granada 64
Capilla Real, Sevilla 20
El Capricho 77
car rental 121
La Carihuela 9, 86–7
El Carmen 44
Carombolo Treasure 82
Cartuja de la Asunción 65
Carvajal 60
Casa del Gigante 74
Casa Manuel de Falla 64
Casa Museo García Lorca 59
Casa Natal Picasso 30
Casa de Pilatos 82
Casa del Rey Moro 74, 76
Casares 18, 79
Casco Antiguo 21
casinos 108
Castillo de Aguila 62
Castillo de Gibralfaro 32
Castillo de San Miguel 42
Castillo de Sohail 60
Catedral, Granada 65
Catedral, Málaga 33
Catedral, Sevilla 20
Centro de Observación Marina 107
ceramics 103

children's attractions 106–7
chiringuitos 72
cinema and theatre 108–9
climate 7, 118, 123
clothing sizes 123
Cofradía del Santo Christo de Amor 21
Columbus, Christopher 20, 51
Competa 50
concessions 123
consulates 120
Convento Real de San Zoilo 45
Córdoba 51–3
Córdoba City Museum 53
Cueva de Menga 44
Cueva de la Pileta 75
Cueva de los Siete Palacios 43
Cuevas de Nerja 19, 70
customs regulations 119

de Falla, Manuel 14, 64
departure information 124
disabilities, travellers with 99
discos 109
drinking water 123
drives
    Andalucían towns 79
    to Antequera 88
    coastal drive to Gibraltar 61
    hill drive to Mijas 49
driving 118, 121
Duquesa Marina 61

Eagle Gardens 106
eating out 54, 72–3, 92–7
electricity 122
emergency telephone numbers 119, 122
La Encarnación 89
entertainment 108–16
Ermita de Nuestro Señor Santiago 21
Estepona 56, 106

famous residents and visitors 14
fashion shopping 102–3
festivals and events 116
Finca de la Concepción Jardín Botánico-Histórico 38
flamenco and jazz 109–10
food and drink 72–3, 92–7
food and wine shops 103–4
Frigiliana 59
Fuengirola 60, 106–7
Fuente Vaqueros 59

Gaucín 62, 79
geography 7
Gibraltar 61
gift shops 104
La Giralda 20
Golden Mile 68
golf 14, 55, 78, 111–12
Granada 63–5, 107
Grazalema 12
green tourism 12

health 118, 123
Hemingway, Ernest 75
hiking 12
history 10–11
horseriding 12, 112–13
hot-air ballooning 110–11
hotel grades 98

Iglesia de la Concepción 23
Iglesia de los Mártires 36
Iglesia del Sagrario 33
Iglesia de San Juan 36
Iglesia de Santiago 36
Iglesia del Santo Cristo de la Salud 36
insurance 118, 123

Jardín de las Aguílas 106
jetskiing 55
jewellery 104–5

Laguna de Fuente de Piedra 13
language 124
leatherware 105
local ways and etiquette 54
Lorca, García 59
Lovers' Rock 88

Málaga 9, 14, 28–39
maps
    Andalucía 42–3
    Costa del Sol 46–7
    Málaga 30–1
Marbella 9, 14, 66–8, 107
Marbella Club 6, 66
markets 55, 105
Maro 70
meal times 96
La Mezquita 22
Mijas 9, 23, 49, 107
Mirador del Ventanillo 44
money 119
Montes de Málaga 88
Motril 70
Museo Arqueológico, Benalmádena Pueblo 47
Museo Arqueológico, Sevilla 82
Museo Arqueológico Provincial, Córdoba 52
Museo Arqueológico Provincial, Granada 65
Museo de Artes y Tradiciones Populares 37
Museo de Bellas Artes, Córdoba 52
Museo de Bellas Artes, Sevilla 83
Museo Histórico 53
Museo Municipal Taurino 53
Museo Provincial de Arqueología 37
musuems 120

National Game Reserve 12
national holidays 120
nature parks and reserves 12
Nerja 69–70
nightlife 108

125

Nuestra Señora de las Nieves 89

Ojén 49
olives 95
opening hours 120
Ornithological Park 42–3

Palacio del Generalife 17, 63
Palacio del Marqués de Salvatierra 74
Palacio de Mondragón 74
Palacio-Museo de Viana 53
para-sailing and hang-gliding 110, 111
paradores 100
Parque Acuático Aquavelis 107
Parque Acuático Mijas 107
Parque de las Ciencias 107
El Parque, Málaga 38
Parque Nacional El Torcal de Antequera 12, 44
Parque Natural Montes de Málaga 12
Parque Natural Sierra de Las Nieves 12
Parque Natural Sierra Nevada 12
Parque Natural del Torcal de Antequera 12, 88
passports and visas 118
Peña de los Enamorados 88
personal safety 122
pharmacies 120, 123
photography 123
Picasso Museum 30
Picasso, Pablo 14, 30, 36
Pileta Cave 75
Pink Lagoon 13
police 122
polo 113
postal services 122

Prado World 106
public transport 121
Puente Nuevo 26
Puerto Banús 9, 24–5, 68, 107
Puerto Sotogrande 61
Punta Marroquí 13

Reales Alcázares 83
El Retiro Jardín Botánico 38
Rilke, Rainer María 75
Rincón de la Victoria 74
Roman Amphitheatre 16
Roman Baths 45
Ronda 9, 26, 74–6, 79
rural accommodation 13, 101

Sacramonte 63
sailing 55, 114
St Michael's Cave 61
Salobreña 77
San Pedro de Alcántara 78
San Roque 78
San Sebastian 18
Santa María la Mayor, Antequera 44
Santa María la Mayor, Vélez-Málaga 90
Santuario de la Victoria 36
Santuario de la Virgen de la Peña Limosnas 23
Science Park 107
scuba diving 55, 114–15
Sea Life Parque Submarino 106
Semana Santa (Holy Week) 116
senior citizens 123
Sevilla 80–3
shopping 102–5, 120
skiing 55, 115
soft drinks 95
Sotogrande 61, 78
spices 7

sport and leisure 7, 14, 55, 110–15
students 123
sun protection 107, 123
Suspiro del Moro 65
swimming 55, 115

tapas 93
Tarifa 84
taxis 121
telephones 122
tennis 14, 55, 113–14
time 118, 119
tipping 122
Tivoli World Show and Amusement Park 47, 106
toilets 121
Torre de la Calahorra 53
Torre del Mar 85, 107
Torremolinos 86–7, 107
Torrox 89
Torrox Costa 89
tourist offices 118, 120
trains 121
travelling to Portugal 119

Vélez-Málaga 90
Verdiales 116
Villa Romano de Río Verde 78

walks
  Antequera 45
  Málaga churches 39
  Málaga old town 35
  Ronda 76
waterskiing 55, 115
watersports 114–15
windsurfing 55, 115
wines and liqueurs 73, 95

Zoológico de Fuengirola 106–7

Acknowledgements
The Automobile Association wishes to thank the following photographers, libraries and associations for their assistance in the preparation of this book: IMAGES COLOUR LIBRARY front cover (b) beach scene; MARY EVANS PICTURE LIBRARY 10, 14a, 14b, 65; MRI BANKERS' GUIDE TO FOREIGN CURRENCY 119; ROBERT HARDING PICTURE LIBRARY front cover (c) spanish lady; SPECTRUM COLOUR LIBRARY 19, 52/3, 83; ZEFA PICTURES LTD 1, 17

The remaining photographs are held in the Association's own library (AA PHOTO LIBRARY) with contributions from P BAKER 122c; J EDMUNSON 5b, 7, 20b, 26, 27a, 32, 51, 53, 63, 84, 87/8; A MOLYNEUX 20a, 41, 80, 82; K PATERSON back cover, oranges; J POULSEN 16, 21, 37a, 37b, 45, 50b, 62, 73a, 75; D ROBERTSON front cover (a) Granada Alhambra, 2, 8a, 8c, 11, 12, 15a, 22, 40, 44, 64; J A TIMS 5a, 6, 8a, 8d, 9a, 9b, 15b, 18, 24, 24/5, 27b, 28, 29, 31, 33a, 34a, 34b, 35, 36, 38, 39, 43, 48, 49, 50a, 54/5, 56, 57, 58, 59a, 61, 66/7, 67a, 68, 69, 70, 71, 72, 74, 77, 78, 79, 85a, 85b, 87, 88, 89a, 89b, 90a, 90b, 91a, 91b, 117b, 122a, 122b; W VOYSEY front cover (d) Mijas, 13, 23, 60, 73b, 76, 117a

Author's Acknowledgements
Mona King would like to thank the Costa del Sol Tourist Board, Torremolinos, the Spanish Tourist Office, London, Hotel Andalucía Plaza, Marbella, El Castillo de Monda, Monda, and Hotel Reina Victoria, Ronda for their assistance with this book.

Contributors
Copy editor: Hilary Hughes Page Layout: Design 23 Verifier: Teresa Fisher
Researcher (Practical Matters): Colin Follett Indexer: Marie Lorimer